The Disciples' Diet Cookbook

Bible-Based Recipes To Help You Feel Energized and Thrive

Chris D. Meletis, N.D.

Kimberly Wilkes

Danielle Heiderich

www.disciplesdiet.com

Disclaimer

The information provided in this book is designed to provide helpful information on the subjects discussed. This book is not meant to be used, nor should it be used, to diagnose or treat any medical condition. For diagnosis or treatment of any medical problem, consult your own physician. Before making any changes to your health and wellness protocol consult your personal provider and pharmacist. The publisher and authors are not responsible for any specific health or allergy needs that may require medical supervision and are not liable for any damages or negative consequences from any treatment, action, application or preparation, to any person reading or following the information in this book.

References are provided for informational purposes only and do not constitute endorsement of any websites or other sources. Readers should be aware that the websites listed in this book may change.

No medical claims or promises are intended to be inferred or made in this publication or related website and educational content. The items discussed in this work are not intended to diagnose, treat, cure, or prevent any disease.

Published internationally by Divine Medicine Press
Portland, Oregon

Introduction

A Cookbook Meant To Help You Have More Energy and Thrive—By Following In Jesus' Culinary Footsteps

Jesus likely ate a very simple diet. He didn't have a lot of money, so unless He was attending a feast, He probably ate a lot of bread and fish. When He attended Passover feasts or other special occasions He probably ate some meat, such as lamb. People in His day often didn't eat lunch.

In the modern world, we're used to eating less simply. Our taste buds are accustomed to more complex and pleasing tastes. In creating the recipes in this book, we believe we've struck a good balance between creating dishes similar to the types of food available in Jesus' time while making them pleasing to the modern palate.

This Is Not A Vegetarian Cookbook—Although Vegans Could Use It

This is not a pesco-vegetarian cookbook. You'll find recipes for some meat dishes. If you are a vegan, there are plenty of recipes where coconut or cashew yogurt or nut milks can replace dairy. In fact, we stay away from cow's milk, for reasons mentioned in *The Disciples Diet* book, which is a companion book to this cookbook. We highly recommend you read it to get a better feel for the way Jesus' ate and lived. (It's available on Amazon.)

It's Not an Exact Replica of Jesus' Eating Habits

We include ingredients in this book that weren't available in the Holy Land of Jesus' time. For example, some recipes have avocados or tomatoes. Jesus ate a primarily low-glycemic diet that didn't cause large spikes in blood sugar. Avocados, tomatoes, and coconut—while not available to Jesus—mirror the way He ate in that they're low glycemic and/or contain nutrients you need to feel your best. For example, avocados contain potassium, tomatoes have lycopene, and coconut milk has a large amount of magnesium and potassium. Jesus' diet also likely had a low glycemic load. We cover the difference between glycemic load and glycemic index in *The Disciples' Diet* book.

Four Things You Must Avoid To Eat—and Live—Like Jesus

To eat like Jesus and His disciples, the three most important things to avoid are highly processed food, sugar, and genetically modified (GMO) ingredients. People in Biblical times did not eat any of these type

Introduction

of foods. They ate fresh, unprocessed food loaded with nutrients. Their food also wasn't covered in toxic pesticides and herbicides. If you're going to use the recipes in this book to feel your best and live longer, it's important to use organic, non-GMO ingredients and avoid sugar and processed foods. We present the research supporting the benefits of organic, non-GMO food in *The Disciples' Diet* book.

Eating the way Jesus ate is a crucial step to feeling energetic and healthy. But there's something else as important: living the way Jesus lived. That's why, for best results, this cookbook is meant to be used together with *The Disciples' Diet* book, which discusses powerful lifestyle changes that must be made in order to live longer and feel healthier.

Eating Healthy Has Never Been More Delicious

We know you'll enjoy the recipes in this book. Eating healthier does not mean you have to sacrifice great-tasting foods. However, it does mean you'll have to give up sugar. Sugar is very addictive. Giving it up may at first be a challenge. Making some of the stevia-sweetened or honey-sweetened recipes in this cookbook will make you feel less deprived. And make sure you never let your blood sugar drop too low by going too long without eating. When your blood sugar drops, you're more likely to reach for unhealthy foods.

As you use this cookbook to become healthier, lose weight, and have more energy, know that you are in our prayers. We believe that God wants us all to live a vibrant life and He's given us a tool to do it—healthy, delicious food.

Table of Contents

Meal Plans

Here are four weeks of suggested meal plans to make it easy for you eat in a way that's similar to Jesus and His disciples. The recipes for the suggested meals are in this cookbook.

Week 1	BREAKFAST	LUNCH	DINNER	DESSERT
Day 1	Gluten-Free Date and Nut Bread	Baba Ganoush with Vegetable Sticks and Gluten-Free Crackers	Skillet Pasta	Grain-Free Peanut Butter Ginger Cookies
Day 2	Gluten-Free Pumpkin Pancakes with Cranberry Apple Compote	Chef Salad	Stuffed Baked Sweet Potato and Grilled Raddichio	
Day 3	Daniel's Veggie Smoothie	Salmon Patties and Garden Salad	Masala Chicken Curry with Steamed Brown Rice and Braised Spinach	Sweet Potato Cranberry Gluten-Free Quick Bread
Day 4	Berry, Pistachio, Yogurt Parfaits	Hummus with Veggie Sticks and Gluten-Free Crackers	Slow Cooker Pot Roast	
Day 5	Raisin Spice Chia Pudding	Chicken and Red Cabbage Slaw with Tahini Dressing	Lemon Dill Cod with Polenta and Broccoli with Cashews and Lemon	
Day 6	Homemade Granola	Quinoa Tabouli Salad	Spaghetti Squash with Chicken, Asparagus, and Marinated Artichokes	
Day 7	Quinoa with Pecans	Savory Vegetable Soup	Skillet Chicken Parmesan with Zoodles and a Garden Salad	Gluten-Free Almond Flour Brownies

Meal Plans

Week 2	BREAKFAST	LUNCH	DINNER	DESSERT
Day 1	Berry Smoothie	Quinoa and Black Bean Salad	Mediterranean Fish Stew	Mixed Fresh Fruit Bowl
Day 2	Crustless Quiche Florentine Cups	Green Pea Soup	Caper Chicken Sauté, Mashed Cauliflower, and Garden Salad	
Day 3	Land of Milk and Honey Overnight Oats	Chick Pea Salad with Mustard Vinaigrette	Salmon with Mustard Yogurt Sauce, Mashed Celeriac, and Steamed Green Beans with Garlic and Almonds	
Day 4	Vegetable and Turkey Ham Omelet	Falafel Wraps with Tzatziki Sauce	Garlic Chicken and Brown Rice	
Day 5	Gluten-Free Date and Nut Muffins	Egg and Endive Salad With Lemon Mustard Vinaigrette	Steamed Fish Steaks, Confetti Rice Salad, and Sautéed Asparagus	
Day 6	Salmon Sausage "Hollandaise" with Dijon Mustard Yogurt Sauce	Beef Stock and Garden Salad	Balsamic Glazed Salmon with Baked Winter Squash and Steamed Brussels Sprouts	2 oz of Dark Chocolate, 85% Cocoa (stevia sweetened if available)
Day 7	Chia Pudding with Blackberries and Blueberries	Chilled Seafood Salad in Lettuce Wraps	Mediterranean Chicken, Broccoli with Cashews and Lemon	

Meal Plans

Week 3	BREAKFAST	LUNCH	DINNER	DESSERT
Day 1	Gluten-Free Breakfast Biscuit Sandwich	Cream of Carrot Soup, Garden Salad	Salmon and Pasta with Lemon Butter Parsley Sauce	
Day 2	Gluten-Free Biscuit and Fruit	Spinach Salad with Strawberries and Cashew, Raisin, and Cinnamon Bread	Roasted Apricot Salmon and Rice	
Day 3	Stuffed Grape Leaves and Hardboiled Eggs	Seasoned Bean and Egg Salad	Balsamic Lamb Chops	
Day 4	Greek Yogurt with Gluten-Free Granola	Broccoli Slaw with Chickpeas	Salmon and Pasta with Lemon Butter Parsley Sauce	Berry Fruit Salad
Day 5	Mediterranean Gluten-Free Breakfast Toast	Gluten-Free Pita Bread Stuffed with Vegetables, Feta, and Hummus	Sweet Potato Rosemary Soup	Fruit Salad with Dates and Mint
Day 6	Sweet Potato Hash Brown Bake	Ginger Beef	Steamed Fish with Butternut Squash and Dates	
Day 7	Gluten-Free Cranberry Scones and "Let There Be Light" Scrambled Eggs	Baked Stuffed Acorn Squash	Poached Fish with Avocado Sauce	

Meal Plans

Week 4	BREAKFAST	LUNCH	DINNER	DESSERT
Day 1	Meat and Bell Pepper Omelet	Shrimp Salad Pitas	Black Bean Soup and Gluten-Free Cornbread	
Day 2	Fruit and Nut Bar	Roasted Mushroom and Pepper Wraps	Roast Leg of Lamb Bandit Style with Mixed Squash and Sweet Potatoes and Braised Collard Greens	
Day 3	Quinoa Hot Cereal	Loaded Chicken Salad	Single Skillet Garden Zucchini "Noodles"	
Day 4	Vegetable and Turkey Ham Omelet	Chickpea and Tomato Salad	Steamed Salmon and Lemon Butter Sauce with Butternut Squash and Dates	
Day 5	Date and Walnut Chia Pudding	Curried Quinoa Salad	Salmon with Pomegranate Salsa	Gluten-Free Tahini Cookies
Day 6	Bear More Fruit Peach and Raspberry Parfait	Chickpea Salad with Mustard Vinaigrette	Fish with Herb Sauce, Brown and Wild Rice Medley, and Mixed Steamed Greens	
Day 7	Kale Smoothie	Egg Salad Wraps	Kofte in Tomato Sauce with Zucchini "Noodles"	

Breakfast

Gluten-Free Pumpkin Pancakes with Cranberry Apple Compote

Fruit and Nut Bars

Bake
30-35 min.

Cool
completely
before cutting

Serves 4

 Ingredients

- 1/4 cup pumpkin seeds
- 2 tbsp whole flax seeds
- 1/4 cup dried cranberries (fruit-juice sweetened)
- 1/4 cup raisins
- 1/4 cup maple syrup or honey
- 2 tbsp almond butter
- 2 tbsp almond flour
- 1/4 teaspoon salt

Instructions

1. Preheat the oven to 300°F.
2. Lightly grease an 8-inch square pan and line with parchment paper.
3. Combine the nuts, seeds, and cranberries in a medium bowl.
4. In a small bowl, whisk together the maple syrup, almond butter, almond flour, and salt until smooth and evenly blended.
5. Pour the wet ingredients into the fruit/nut mixture and stir until evenly moistened.
6. Spoon the mixture into the prepared pan, pressing it down firmly to smooth.
7. Bake 30 to 35 minutes. Cool completely before cutting. Makes 4 servings.

Quinoa with Pecans

Serves 2

Quinoa is not a food that Jesus ate. It originated in South America. But it fits the qualifications for a Disciples' Diet type food. It's high in protein and has a low glycemic index. So it will fill you up without causing a huge spike in your blood sugar.

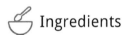 Ingredients

- 1 cup quinoa
- 2 1/4 cups nut milk
- 1 tsp cinnamon
- 1 tsp butter
- 1 tsp natural maple extract
- 1/2 cup pecan halves

Instructions

1. Roast pecan halves in a 325°F oven for 15 minutes.

2. Set aside to cool.

3. Cook quinoa in nut milk until the liquid is absorbed about 20 minutes.

4. Remove from heat and fluff with fork.

5. Immediately add cinnamon, butter, and maple extract.

6. Spoon quinoa into two dishes and sprinkle pecan halves over each dish. Serves 2.

Kale Smoothie

Kale has roots in the Mediterranean and Turkey, where it was grown for food starting around 2,000 BC. People in Greece were also growing flat-leafed varieties in the 4th century BC. Its presence in that part of the world suggests that Jesus and His contemporaries were eating this vegetable.

Serves 2

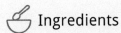

Ingredients

- 2 cups packed organic kale, torn into pieces
- 1 stalk celery, chopped
- 3/4 cup almond milk
- 1/2 sweet apple, cored and rough chopped
- 1 tsp lemon juice
- 1-2 tsp raw local honey to taste
- 3/4 cup ice

Instructions

1. Blend all ingredients together until smooth.
2. Add more almond milk if needed to thin the mixture to the desired consistency.

Berry, Pistachio, and Yogurt Parfaits

Serves 2

Even though Jesus likely did not eat coconut, it's a healthy food and a great replacement for dairy. It's a good option for vegans. So you will see coconut turn up in a number of recipes in this book. This recipe also includes pistachios, which are native to the Middle East and were therefore likely a part of Jesus' diet.

 Ingredients

- 1 cup grass fed unsweetened yogurt or coconut yogurt
- 1 tsp vanilla
- 2 cup berries
- 2 tbsp chopped pistachios
- 1/2 tsp cinnamon

 Instructions

1. Place yogurt in bowl and stir in the vanilla.
2. Place 1/4 cup yogurt on the bottom of each of two wine glasses or small parfait dishes.
3. Place 1/4 cup berries on top of the yogurt in each glass or dish.
4. Divide the remaining 1/2 cup yogurt into each glass or dish.
5. Place the remaining berries on top of the yogurt in each dish or glass.
6. Sprinkle each parfait with 1 tbsp chopped nuts and a 1/4 tsp cinnamon.

Gluten-Free Date and Nut Muffins

Bake
35-40 min.

Cool in the
pan 15 min.

Makes
12 muffins

Although Jesus ate wheat, the type of wheat people ate during that time was very different from the type of wheat we eat today. Because today's wheat is not as healthy, the recipes in this book call for gluten-free flour. We also recommend you experiment with cooking with einkorn wheat and barley, which are more similar to grains Jesus consumed. Read *The Disciples' Diet* to learn more about this type of wheat. This recipe—and a number in the book—uses stevia. Jesus and our Biblical ancestors didn't eat stevia. However, we like to limit honey intake since it spikes blood sugar and contains fructose. Unless fructose is accompanied by fiber, it damages the liver over time. Organic stevia is a healthy replacement.

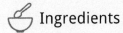 Ingredients

- 3 cups blanched almond flour
- 1/2 tsp sea salt
- 1/2 tsp baking soda
- 1/4 tsp ground nutmeg
- 1/4 tsp cinnamon
- 1/4 cup melted butter
- 2 tbsp organic stevia
- 2 large eggs
- 1 tbsp vanilla extract
- 2 medium apples, peeled, cored, and sliced
- 1 cup chopped pecans
- 1/2 cup dates, chopped into small pieces

Instructions

1. Preheat the oven to 350 degrees F.

2. Line 12 muffin cups with paper muffin liners or grease the cups well.

3. Whisk together the almond flour, salt, baking soda, nutmeg, and cinnamon in a large bowl.

4. In a blender, mix together melted butter, stevia, eggs, vanilla extract, and apples until smooth.

5. Combine the wet ingredients with the almond flour mixture. Fold in the dates and pecans. Spoon the batter into the muffin cups.

6. Bake for 35 to 45 minutes. The muffin tops should be golden brown and a toothpick inserted in the center should be clean when removed. Let the muffins cool in the pan for 15 minutes. Makes 12 muffins.

Salmon Sausage "Hollandaise" with Dijon Mustard Yogurt Sauce

Serves 2

 Ingredients

- 1 package of 6 Vital Choice Savory Country Style Salmon Sausages available at www.vitalchoice.com
- 1/2 cup fresh spinach
- 3 tbsp olive oil
- 3/4 cup grass fed yogurt
- 6 tbsp Dijon mustard

This recipe goes well with sweet potatoes chopped into half inch pieces and sautéed in olive oil.

Instructions

1. Chop spinach and sauté it in olive oil.

2. Cook the salmon sausage according to package directions.

3. Arrange two sausages each on three plates and spoon the spinach over the sausages.

4. Place the yogurt and Dijon mustard into a small pot. Cook on low heat, stirring constantly, just until the mixture is warm. Don't let it boil.

5. Pour the yogurt-mustard mixture over the sausage and spinach. Serves 2.

Why Choosing Organic Stevia Is Important

Like anything else we put into our bodies, choosing organic stevia helps reduce our pesticide and herbicide burden. Jesus and His contemporaries weren't exposed to these toxic substances. One other reason it's important to choose organic Stevia? Stevia often contains erythritol, which is made from corn. Most corn is genetically modified (GM). We talk about the hazards of GM foods in our *Disciples' Diet* book.

Stuffed Grape Leaves and Hardboiled Eggs

Serves 12

 Ingredients

- 1 cup short-grain brown rice
- 2 cups water or chicken broth
- 1 medium-onion chopped
- 1/2 cup chopped fresh dill
- 1/2 cup chopped fresh mint
- 1 cup fresh lemon juice
- 60 organic grape leaves (1, 16 oz jar), drained and rinsed
- Olive oil
- 12 eggs

Instructions

1. Cook the rice according to package directions using either the water or chicken broth. When it's finished cooking, set aside for ten minutes.

2. Sauté the onion, dill, and mint, about five minutes or until the onion is soft. Combine this mixture with the rice. Add ½ cup of the lemon juice.

3. To stuff the leaves, face the shiny side downwards, and place 1 teaspoon of the rice mixture by the bottom stem end of the leaf. Fold over both ends of each leaf towards the center. Roll up from the stem to the top and set into a 4-quart pot. Make sure there are no gaps between the leaves as you place them in the pot, otherwise the stuffing will spill out when cooking.

Sprinkle with the remaining 1/2 cup lemon juice and the cup of olive oil. Pour 1 1/2 cups boiling water over the grape leaves. Cover pot and simmer for about 30 minutes. Do not let pot come to a boil, otherwise the stuffing could escape from the leaves. Remove from heat, uncover, and let cool for about 30 minutes.

4. While the pot is simmering, place 12 eggs in a large pot filled with water. Bring to a boil, turn off heat, and cover. Let sit on burner for 20 minutes. Remove from burner, fill the pot with cold water, let sit for five minutes, then peel the eggs and put on a platter or in a bowl. Arrange the grape leaves on another platter. Serves 12.

Quinoa Hot Cereal

Serves 2

 Ingredients

- 1 cup quinoa
- 2 1/4 cups almond milk
- 1 tbsp organic stevia
- 1 tsp cinnamon
- 1/4 tsp nutmeg
- 1/2 tsp salt
- 1/2 cup chopped nuts
- 1 cup fresh fruit such as blueberries, apples, bananas, or figs or 1/2 cup dried fruit such as raisins, dried cranberries, or dates
- 1/2 cup chopped nuts

Instructions

1. Cook 2 cups quinoa in almond milk until liquid is almost absorbed, about 15 minutes.

2. Add sweetener, spices, and fruit. Cook another 5 minutes or until liquid is completely absorbed.

3. Add optional mix-ins and up to 1/4 cup additional almond milk if desired. Serves 2.

Raisin Spice Chia Pudding

Serves 4

 Ingredients

- 2 cups full fat coconut milk
- 1/2 cup chia seeds
- 1/2 tsp vanilla extract
- 1/4 cup organic stevia sweetener or honey
- 1/2 tsp cinnamon powder
- 1/2 cup raisins
- 1/4 cup boiling water
- 1/8 tsp nutmeg
- 1/8 tsp cloves
- Pinch of salt

Instructions

1. In a medium bowl pour boiling water over raisins. Soak for 20 minutes to plump raisins. Drain and squeeze out water.

2. Add all other ingredients to a blender and blend for 1-2 minutes until smooth.

3. Pour into the medium bowl, and stir to distribute raisins.

4. Divide into 4 portions in small airtight containers. Refrigerate overnight, stirring a few times in the first hour to maintain even thickening. Serves 4.

Bear More Fruit Peach and Raspberry Yogurt Parfait

Serves 1

 Ingredients

- 5 oz unsweetened grass fed yogurt or coconut yogurt
- 1 cup fresh peaches, sliced
- 1/2 cup fresh raspberries
- 2 tbsp gluten-free, unsweetened granola (buy in the store or use the recipe later in this cookbook

Instructions

1. In a parfait glass or small bowl layer yogurt with peaches and raspberries. Top with granola. Serves 1.

Gluten-Free
Cranberry Scones

Bake
15-20 min.

Serves 6

Ingredients

- 1 3/4 cups gluten-free baking mix 2 tbsp organic stevia
- 2 tbsp honey
- 2 tsp baking powder
- 1/2 tsp salt
- 1/4 cup chilled coconut oil or butter
- 1/4 cup unsweetened apple sauce
- 3/4 cup dried fruit-juice sweetened cranberries
- 2 tbsp orange zest
- 2 large egg
- 1/3 cup chilled full fat coconut milk*
- 1 tsp vanilla extract
- 1/2 tsp orange extract

Instructions

1. Preheat oven to 400 degrees F. Line a baking sheet with parchment paper and grease the parchment paper.

2. Whisk together flour, salt, sweeteners, and baking powder. Cut in the chilled coconut oil or butter and apple sauce until the mixture is crumbly. Stir in orange zest and dried fruit.

3. Whisk together the eggs, milk, and extracts, beating well. Add to the dry ingredients and stir until well combined. Mix should be very sticky.

4. Drop by 1/3 cups on baking sheet 2 inches apart. Refrigerate for 25 minutes before baking to chill the fats.

5. Bake for 15 to 20 minutes until golden brown. Let rest at least 5 minutes before serving.

*When using coconut milk for baking be sure to choose full fat coconut milk without added stabilizers or emulsifiers. Refrigerate canned coconut milk overnight before using. Remove from the refrigerator and open carefully without tipping. Scrape the solids off the top for use in your recipe and reserve the water that has collected in the bottom of the can for other uses, like smoothies. Use BPA-free canned coconut milk.

Gluten-Free Biscuits

Bake
15 min.

Serves 12

 Ingredients

- 1 3/4 cups gluten free cup for cup flour blend
- 1/4 cup cornstarch
- 1 tbsp baking powder
- 1/4 tsp baking soda
- 1/2 tsp kosher salt
- 2 tsp honey
- 8 tbsp unsalted butter, cubed
- 1 cup almond milk + 1 tbsp white vinegar
- 1 tbsp melted butter

Instructions

1. Preheat oven to 425 degrees F. Line a baking sheet with parchment paper and grease paper.

2. In a large bowl, whisk together the dry ingredients. Cut in the chilled butter. Add the milk and vinegar and mix until just combined.

3. Drop batter by 1/4 cup portions on the baking sheet using two large spoons. Press tops lightly to flatten and brush with melted butter.

4. Bake 15 minutes until golden brown. Allow to rest 5-10 minutes before serving.

Sweet Potato Hashbrown Bake

Serves 6

Sweet potatoes are native to either tropical South or Central America, so Jesus likely did not have access to these tasty tubers. Growing on a vine in the morning glory family, sweet potatoes have been domesticated in Central America for thousands of years. Even though they're not a food Jesus probably ate, they're a healthy food rich in vitamins A, B6, and E, as well as potassium and fiber, so we're including them in some recipes in this book. However, baked sweet potatoes should be eaten sparingly, since baking a sweet potato increases both the glycemic index and glycemic load. Boiled sweet potatoes have a lower glycemic index and glycemic load. For more information about glycemic index and load, we recommend you read *The Disciples' Diet* book.

 Ingredients

- 2 large sweet potatoes, shredded
- 1 medium onion, diced
- 1 medium yellow bell pepper, diced
- 1 lb turkey sausage, cooked and crumbled
- 6 eggs
- 8 oz button mushrooms, sliced
- 1 tsp dried thyme
- 3 tbsp olive oil
- Salt and pepper to taste.
- Non-stick olive oil cooking spray or oil mister

☺ Instructions

1. Shred sweet potatoes with a food processor, mandolin, or spiralizer.

2. In a large saucepan heat 1 tbsp oil over medium heat. Add onion and bell pepper and sauté until almost soft about 5 minutes. Add mushrooms and cook another 2 minutes.

3. Pour into a large mixing bowl. Add another 2 tbsp oil to the skillet and gently cook sweet potatoes for 10 minutes until soft. Add to mixing bowl.

4. Add sausage to skillet, cooking until meat is thoroughly browned, breaking up sausage into small crumbles as it cooks. Drain excess fat and then add sausage to bowl. Sprinkle thyme over the top, add salt and pepper to taste and mix thoroughly.

5. Preheat oven to 375 degrees F.

6. Grease a 9 x 13 pan with oil or non-stick olive oil cooking spray and pour in hash. Slip into the oven to brown.

7. Meanwhile grease a 6-cup muffin tin and crack one egg into each cup. Sprinkle with a little salt and pepper.

8. Once hash has been in the oven for 10 minutes place the eggs in the oven as well, and bake another 12-15 minutes for eggs with runny yolks, or add another 3 minutes for soft set yolks. Remove both pans from the oven.

9. To serve divide hash onto 6 plates and carefully place 1 egg on top, breaking the yolk to allow the creamy goodness to cover the hash browns. Serves 6.

Gluten-Free Breakfast Biscuit Sandwiches

Serves 4

A traditional breakfast sandwich doesn't include any vegetables. We've added baby spinach to boost the nutrient content of this breakfast favorite.

 Ingredients

- 4 gluten-free biscuits (see gluten-free biscuit recipe in the breakfast section)
- 4 eggs
- 4 turkey sausage patties
- 4 thin slices raw milk organic cheddar cheese
- A handful of baby spinach

Instructions

1. Hard fry eggs in a medium skillet.

2. Sauté turkey sausage patties until well done. Drain well on paper towels.

3. To assemble, split biscuits in half. Place an egg, a sausage patty, and a slice of cheese on half of each biscuit. If necessary, place under broiler for 1 minute to melt the cheese.

4. Place a little of the baby spinach on each sandwich. Put tops back on. Serves 4.

Land of Milk and Honey Overnight Oats

Serves 4

 Ingredients

- 1/3 cup steel cut oats
- 1/3 cup almond or cashew milk
- 1/3 cup grass fed unsweetened yogurt or kefir
- 1 medium apple, sliced
- 1/4 tsp cinnamon, or more to taste
- Pinch of nutmeg
- Pinch of cloves
- 1 tsp organic stevia or 1 tsp honey
- 1 tsp coconut oil
- 1 tbsp chopped walnuts

Instructions

1. In a small skillet, fry apples in coconut oil for 2-3 minutes to soften.

2. Add spices and stevia or honey, continue to fry for an additional minute.

3. Remove from heat and allow to cool.

4. Combine all ingredients except nuts in a 2-cup container and mix well.

5. Cover tightly and place in the refrigerator overnight.

6. Add crushed nuts just before eating.

Berry Smoothie

Serves 1

 Ingredients

- 1/2 cup each frozen blackberries, raspberries, blueberries and strawberries
- 1/2 cup unsweetened almond or cashew milk
- 1 scoop vanilla protein powder
- 1/2 cup ice

Instructions

1. Place all ingredients in a blender. Blend until smooth, 1-2 minutes.

"Let There Be Light" Scrambled Eggs

Serves 6

No one can say for sure whether Jesus actually ate eggs. They are mentioned a few times in the Bible, at least once as a reference to them as a food. Jesus' contemporaries likely ate them because they're mentioned in the Jewish Code of Law. They were considered a neutral food that is neither dairy nor meat. They were likely more frequently served on the tables of well-to-do people. Nevertheless, they're a low-glycemic, high-protein food, so we are including them in recipes in this book.

 ## Ingredients

- 6 large eggs
- 1/4 cup unsweetened non-dairy milk of your choice
- 1 tbsp olive oil
- 2 tbsp minced fresh herbs
For best flavor, we recommend a combination of herbs be used. Consider herbs such as oregano, cilantro basil, parsley, tarragon, thyme, sage, or marjoram.
- 2 tbsp fresh minced chives
- 1/2 tsp salt
- Fresh cracked black pepper

Instructions

1. In a large mixing bowl, beat eggs with milk and salt until well blended.

2. Heat olive oil in a large skillet over low heat. Pour in eggs. Stir slowly with a spatula until curds start to form.

3. When eggs are still slightly raw but set sprinkle herbs and chives over the top and fold in.

4. Continue to cook until eggs are still soft but not runny or raw looking. Serve immediately. Serves 6.

Daniel's Veggie Smoothie

Serves 2

In the Bible, Daniel asked the steward to put the servants on only vegetables and water for ten days and then compare their appearances with the young men eating the royal food. The men eating the vegetables looked much healthier than those eating the royal food. If Daniel could have made a smoothie at that time, here is what it might have been like. We did add some blueberries for their antioxidant power and a 1/2 orange to make the taste more enjoyable for people not used to having vegetable smoothies.

 Ingredients

- 1 cup packed kale, torn into pieces
- 1 cup fresh spinach
- 1/4 avocado
- 1/4 cup blueberries
- 3/4 cup unsweetened almond or any non-dairy milk
- 1/2 of an orange
- 1 tsp raw local honey
- 1 cup ice

Instructions

1. Blend all ingredients together until smooth. Add more almond milk if needed to thin the mixture to the desired consistency.

Date and Walnut Chia Pudding

Serves 4

 Ingredients

- 2 cups full fat coconut milk
- 1/2 cup chia seeds
- 1/2 tsp vanilla extract
- 1/4 tsp each ground ginger and ground cardamom
- 1 cup dates, divided
- 1/2 cup chopped walnuts
- 1/4 cup boiling water
- Pinch of salt

Instructions

1. Hydrate 1/4 cup dates in 1/4 cup boiling water for 15 minutes. Drain excess water.

2. Add hydrated dates, coconut milk, chia seeds, vanilla, salt, and spices to a blender and blend for 1-2 minutes until smooth.

3. Divide into 4 portions in small airtight containers.

4. Refrigerate overnight, stirring a few times in the first hour to maintain even thickening.

5. Chop remaining dates and walnuts and mix to combine.

6. In the morning top each pudding with 1/4 of the mixed dates and walnuts and stir to combine.

Crustless Quiche Florentine Cups

Bake
15 min.

Serves 6

Although quiche originated in France, the version below is a high-protein, low-glycemic dish. The goal of the *Disciples' Diet* is to get people to give up sugar and processed food and eat a low-glycemic diet. The quiche recipe below, which eliminates the crust, pushes this quiche even lower on the glycemic index. It's so satisfying that when you're done eating it you won't crave any sugary breakfast items like muffins or cinnamon rolls.

 ## Ingredients

- 4 eggs
- 2 cups unsweetened nut milk
- 1/2 tsp salt
- 1/4 tsp pepper
- 3 cups fresh spinach
- 1/2 tsp grated nutmeg
- 1/2 cup finely grated organic raw milk swiss cheese

 ## Instructions

1. In a skillet sauté spinach until wilted, adding 1 tbsp of water if necessary. Place spinach on a clean lint free towel and squeeze out excess liquid. Transfer to a cutting board and chop fine.

2. In a medium mixing bowl whisk together eggs, milk, salt, pepper, and nutmeg.

3. Preheat oven to 350 degrees F. Spray a 6 count muffin tin with nonstick cooking spray. Divide egg mix between all 6 cups. Divide spinach into 6 portions and add to the middle of the cups. Sprinkle each with 1 tbsp plus 1 tsp cheese. Bake until egg mix is set, around 15 minutes. Serves 6.

Vegetable and Turkey Ham Omelet

Serves 4

Jesus very likely ate kosher food as it was the custom among His people. That means he did not eat pork. In this omelet recipe we replaced the pork with turkey ham.

 Ingredients

- 6 eggs
- 1/2 cup each diced onions, bell peppers, baby spinach, and turkey ham
- Salt and Pepper
- 1 tbsp olive oil, divided
- 1 tbsp water

Instructions

1. In a medium skillet sauté onions and peppers in 1 tsp olive oil 2-3 minutes. Add turkey ham and cook for an additional 2 minutes.

2. In a separate bowl whisk eggs, water, salt, and pepper together.

3. Transfer ham and vegetables to a bowl.

4. Add remaining 2 tsp oil to skillet. Add eggs and cook 2 minutes stirring a couple of times to allow eggs to cook through.

5. When the edges are set but the middle is a bit loose add the filling to one side and fold in half. Cook an additional 1 minute per side to set the eggs. Serves 4.

Meat and Bell Pepper Omelet

Serves 4

 ## Ingredients

- 6 eggs 1/4 cup water
- 1/2 cup onion
- 1/2 cup bell pepper
- 4 oz lean ground beef, venison, or bison
- 1/4 tsp salt
- 1/4 tsp pepper
- Olive oil non-stick cooking spray

Instructions

1. Spray a medium skillet with non-stick cooking spray. Sauté meat until browned and move to a separate bowl.

2. Use the pan drippings to sauté onion and pepper until soft, about 5 minutes and add to the bowl with the ground meat.

3. Beat egg and water together until light and foamy and pour into hot skillet. Season with salt and pepper. Stir in the pan until eggs are about half cooked.

4. Pour meat and vegetables onto one half of the omelet and cover tightly. Continue to cook on low heat until eggs are set.

5. If the top isn't set well place under broiler for 1-2 minutes. Slide out of the skillet and flip in half. Serves 4.

Gluten-Free Date and Nut Bread

 Bake
45-50 min.

 Cool
10 min.

Serves 5

Ingredients

- 1/2 stick (4 tbsp) unsalted butter
- 1 cup pitted, coarsely chopped dates
- 1/2 cup organic stevia or honey
- 3/4 cup boiling water
- 1 egg beaten
- 2 cups gluten-free flour
- 2 tsp cinnamon
- 2 tsp baking powder
- 1/2 tsp salt
- 1/2 cup coarsely chopped walnuts
- 1/2 tsp vanilla extract

Instructions

1. Preheat oven to 350 degrees F. Grease a large loaf pan.

2. Cut butter into 7 pieces and place in a large bowl. Put dates on top and then pour the stevia or honey over the dates and butter. Pour boiling water over the mixture and let stand for 7 minutes then stir well.

3. After the mixture has cooled, add the egg and mix well.

4. In a separate bowl, combine flour, cinnamon, baking powder, and salt. Combine with date mixture and beat for 30 seconds.

5. Stir in nuts and vanilla. Pour into the greased pan.

6. Bake for about 45 to 50 minutes until a toothpick inserted into the center comes out clean. Cool on a rack for ten minutes. Remove from pan on to a rack until cooled.

Mediterranean Gluten-Free Breakfast Bread

 Bake
6-8 min.

 Serves 2

Ingredients

- 4 thick slices of gluten-free bread (we like Against the Grain bread available at Whole Foods Market)
- A few drizzles of olive oil
- 1/2 cup hummus (either store bought or see the recipe in this cookbook)
- 1/4 cup baby spinach
- 1 heirloom tomato, chopped into 1/2 inch pieces
- 2 tbsp chopped olives
- 4 tsp feta cheese

Instructions

1. Place bread slices in glass pan, drizzle them with olive oil, and place in oven at 325 degrees for 6 - 8 minutes, depending on how toasty you want your bread.

2. Spread 2 tbsp of hummus on each bread slice. Top each slice with a little baby spinach, tomato pieces, chopped olives, and 1 tsp of feta cheese. Serves 2.

Gluten-Free Pumpkin Pancakes with Cranberry Apple Compote

Serves 4

 Ingredients

- 1 cup gluten-free flour
- 1 tbsp aluminum-free baking powder
- 1 tsp stevia
- 1/4 tsp salt
- 1/2 cup flaxseed meal
- 1 tsp cinnamon or pumpkin pie spices
- 2 eggs beaten (or eggs substitute)
- 1/2 cup unsweetened grass-fed yogurt or unsweetened cashew or coconut yogurt
- 1/2 cup pumpkin
- 1/2 cup grass-fed milk or nut milk
- 1 tsp vanilla extract
- 3 tbsp salted butter, melted

For the compote:

- 1, 12 oz. package organic frozen or fresh cranberries
- 2 organic apples
- 2 organic peaches or apricots
- 3 tbsp organic stevia

Instructions for the Compote

1. Chop the apples into half-inch cubes. Place in pot with cranberries. Add stevia. Pour enough water to cover the fruit and simmer partially covered on lowest heat until much of the liquid is evaporated and the mixture thickens. Keep warm until serving.

Instructions for the Pancakes

1. Mix together the gluten-free flour, stevia, baking powder, salt, and cinnamon or pumpkin pie spice in a bowl. In another bowl, add the melted butter to the pumpkin, then mix in the egg, yogurt, pumpkin, milk and vanilla. Combine and add additional milk if necessary to make a thick batter and let stand for five to ten minutes.

2. Meanwhile, grease a griddle or skillet with butter. Pour the batter onto the griddle or skillet using a ladle. Flip the pancakes when bubbles have formed on the surface. Remove from cooking surface after the other side is golden brown. Serves 4.

Homemade Granola

Bake
30 min.

Serves 4

We recommend using the wild blueberries for this recipe from Vital Choice rather than the cultivated kind found in grocery stores. Wild blueberries are more similar to what Jesus and His disciples ate. Plus, they have a higher antioxidant content.

 Ingredients

- 2 Cups Rolled Oats
- 1/2 cup chopped cashews or almonds
- 1/2 cup nut butter (cashew or almond butter are good choices)
- 1/4 cup sesame seeds
- Frozen wild blueberries (available from Vital Choice, www.vitalchoice.com)

Instructions

1. Grease a 9 x 13 inch glass casserole dish.

2. In a bowl, combine the oats, chopped nuts, nut butter, and sesame seeds.

3. With a spoon, drop the mixture into the casserole dish.

4. Bake at 300 degrees F for a half hour stirring occasionally. Let cool. Place in bowls, top with berries and nut milk.

Breads

Grain-Free Cashew, Raisin, and Cinnamon Bread

Grain-Free Cashew, Raisin, and Cinnamon Bread

Bake 45 min.   Cool 10 min.   Serves 5

This delightful bread has no grains of any kind. It's made with cashew butter and eggs. And it's very easy and fast to prepare. We included cinnamon because cinnamon balances blood sugar. Plus, it's tasty, too. Raisins add a little color and sweetness. Our Biblical ancestors likely ate raisins, which were discovered by accident as early as 2000 BC when ancient farmers found dried grapes growing on vines. Farmers in Turkey, Iran, and Iraq began trading raisins with Greece and Rome, where these dried fruits were highly prized. Although we included this cashew bread in the meal plans as an accompaniment to the spinach and strawberry salad for lunch, it's great for breakfast, too. In fact, it makes a phenomenal French toast! We bet it would make an awesome bread pudding, although we haven't tried doing that yet.

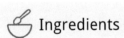 Ingredients

- 1 cup cashew butter
- 5 large organic eggs
- 1 tbsp apple cider vinegar
- 1 tsp cinnamon
- 1 tbsp honey or stevia
- 3/4 tsp baking soda
- 1/4 tsp sea salt
- 1/4 cup organic, unsweetened raisins

Instructions

1. In a blender, pulse cashew butter and eggs until smooth. Stir a few times in between pulses.

2. Add apple cider vinegar, baking soda, salt, honey or stevia, and cinnamon. Stir a few times with a spoon.

3. Combine using the puree or mix setting. Stir in raisins.

4. Pour into a greased 9 x 5 inch loaf dish. Bake at 350 degrees for 45 minutes or until toothpick inserted in center comes out clean.

5. Cool for 10 minutes in the pan then turn out onto a wire rack. Cool for an hour and serve. Serves 5.

Lemon-Blueberry Quick Bread

Bake
60 min.

Cool
20 min.

Serves 4

You can eat this sweet-tangy bread as either a dessert or for breakfast.

Ingredients

- 1/4 cup fresh lemon juice
- 3/4 cup grass fed yogurt
- 1 tsp grated lemon rind
- 2 cups gluten-free flour
- 1 tsp baking powder
- 1/2 tsp salt
- 6 tbsp butter softened
- 1/2 cup organic stevia or honey
- 2 large eggs
- 1/2 cup blueberries

Instructions

1. Preheat oven to 350 degrees. Grease an 8 ½ inch x 4 ½ inch loaf pan.

2. Combine the yogurt, lemon juice, and lemon rind in a small bowl and set aside.

3. In a medium bowl, whisk together the flour, baking powder, and salt and set aside.

4. In a large bowl, beat the butter and stevia or honey until combined. Add the eggs one at a time, beating after each addition. Combine the dry ingredients with the butter mixture alternating with the yogurt mixture.

5. Pour into the loaf pan. Bake for about an hour or until a cake tester or small knife inserted in the middle comes out clean. Cool the bread in the pan for 10 minutes. Remove from pan onto a cooling rack.

6. Although it will be difficult to resist gobbling up a slice or two of the sweet-smelling bread at this point, let cool for at least 20 minutes before slicing. This keeps it from falling apart.

Sweet Potato Cranberry Gluten-Free Quick Bread

Bake 60 min.   Cool 10 min.   Serves 6-8

This delicious treat is another quick bread that you can eat as a dessert or for breakfast. Using stevia rather than sugar or honey keeps it lower on the glycemic index.

 Ingredients

- 1/2 cup melted butter
- 1/2 cup organic stevia
- 1 egg
- 2 cups gluten-free flour
- 1 tsp baking powder
- 1 tsp baking soda
- 1 tsp pumpkin pie spice
- 1/8 tsp salt
- 1 cup mashed organic sweet potatoes
- 1/2 cup fresh or frozen cranberries
- 1/2 cup chopped pecans

Instructions

1. Preheat oven to 350 degrees. Grease a 9 x 5-inch glass loaf pan.

2. In a large bowl, beat the butter, stevia, and egg until blended. Add the flour, baking powder, soda, pumpkin pie spice, salt, and sweet potatoes. Fold in the cranberries and pecans.

3. Pour the batter into the loaf pan. Bake for 1 hour or until a cake tester or butter knife inserted in the center comes out clean.

4. Cool bread in the pan for 10 minutes. Remove from pan and cool on a wire rack for an additional 10 minutes. Serves 6 - 8.

Gluten-Free Cornbread

Bake
20-30 min.

Serves 6-8

Corn was not a part of Jesus' diet. It originated in Mexico. However, *The Disciples' Diet* is a low-glycemic diet and corn meets that criteria. As long as you don't have a food intolerance to corn and as long as you eat organic corn to avoid GMOs, a limited amount of corn is healthy. For more about food intolerances, read *The Disciples' Diet* book.

 Ingredients

- 1 1/2 cups organic ground yellow cornmeal
- 1/2 cup organic flaxseed meal
- 1 tsp salt
- 1 tsp baking soda
- 2 tsp baking powder
- 2 eggs, beaten
- 1 1/2 cups organic grassfed yogurt
- 4 tablespoons pasture butter, melted
- 1/2 cup organic unsweetened coconut milk
- 4 tablespoons (84 g) honey

Instructions

1. Preheat oven to 400 degrees. Lightly grease an 8 X 8 glass baking dish.

2. In a medium mixing bowl whisk together dry ingredients.

3. Mix the beaten eggs and yogurt together. Add the coconut milk and melted butter and blend well.

4. Pour the wet ingredients in with the dry and beat together until smooth.

5. Bake for 20-30 minutes until a toothpick inserted in the middle comes out clean.

....

"For the Lord your God brings
you into a good land, a land of
brooks of water, of fountains and
depths that spring out of valleys
and hills; A land of wheat, and
barley, and vines, and fig trees, and
pomegranates; a land of oil olive,
and honey; A land wherein you
shall eat bread without scarceness,
you shall not lack any thing in it."

Deuteronomy 7 9 NIV

....

Lunch

Savory Vegetable Soup

Salmon Patties

Cook
3 min./side

Makes 8-10
patties

 Ingredients

- 2 BPA-free cans of wild salmon, 7.5 ounces each
- 1 large egg
- 1/4 cup chopped red onion
- 1 cup gluten-free bread crumbs sweetened with honey or unsweetened
- 2 tbsp chopped fresh dill
- 1 tbsp fresh lemon juice
- 1 tsp Dijon mustard
- 1 tsp lemon zest

Instructions

1. Cover bottom of a skillet with olive oil and preheat on medium heat.

2. Remove the bones from the salmon.

3. In a bowl, combine the salmon with the other ingredients.

4. Shape into small patties and place on the preheated skillet.

5. Brown the patties, cooking about 3 minutes each side.

6. Remove patties from skillet onto a serving platter. Makes about 8 - 10 patties.

Gluten-Free Pita Bread Stuffed with Vegetables, Feta, and Hummus

Serves 2

People in the Middle East have been eating pita bread for thousands of years. The pocket pita, which many people are more familiar with than the pocketless variety, was introduced in the 1980s. This recipe presumes you're using pitas without the pockets.

 Ingredients

- 2 gluten-free pita bread slices (We like Against the Grain pita bread)
- 1/2 cup hummus (either store bought or use the recipe in this book)
- 2 tbsp feta
- 1/4 cup olive oil + 3 tbsp
- 1/4 cup balsamic vinegar
- 1/2 red pepper
- 1/2 yellow pepper
- 8 mushrooms
- 3 tbs olive oil

Instructions

1. Dice red pepper and yellow pepper.
2. Sauté peppers in skillet with 3 tbsp of the olive oil and mushrooms until soft. Mix remaining 1/4 cup olive oil with vinegar.
3. Warm the pita bread in a 300 degree F oven for 5 minutes.
4. Place 1/4 cup hummus and 1 tbsp feta on top of each pita. Top each pita with half the pepper and mushroom mixture. Pour oil and vinegar over vegetables. Fold over or roll the pita bread to create sandwiches. Serves 2.

Shrimp Salad Pitas

Serves 5

 Ingredients

- 1 lb cooked pink shrimp (Vital Choice is a good brand, www.vitalchoice.com)
- 5 gluten-free pita bread slices (We like Against the Grain pita bread)
- 1 celery stalk
- 2 tbsp olive oil
- Juice of one lemon
- 1 small garlic clove
- 1 pint grape tomatoes
- 1 small bunch spinach, stems removed
- 1/8 tsp sea salt
- 1/2 cup unsweetened plain grass-fed yogurt or coconut yogurt

 Instructions

1. Chop celery and spinach into small pieces and mince the garlic clove. Place in bowl.

2. Cut the grape tomatoes in half and add to bowl along with the lemon juice, sea salt, and yogurt. Stir to combine. Add shrimp.

3. Warm the pita bread in a 300 degree F oven for 5 minutes.

4. Divide the mixture and spread on the pita slices. Roll up or fold in half. Serves 5.

Loaded Chicken Salad

Bake
15 min.

Serves 4

Ingredients

- 2 large organic, free range chicken breasts, chopped into 1-inch cubes
- 2 cups seedless grapes, halved
- 1/4 cup dried fruit-juice sweetened cranberries
- 1/4 cup chopped nuts
- 1 cup chopped celery
- 2 medium apples, cored and diced
- 1 tsp each onion powder, garlic powder, dried Italian seasoning
- 1 tbsp olive oil
- Salt and pepper
- 1/4 cup honey-sweetened mayonnaise
- 1/4 cup plain grass fed yogurt
- 1/4 cup chicken broth

Instructions

1. Preheat oven to 400 degrees F.

2. In a medium bowl combine olive oil, onion powder, garlic powder, and Italian seasoning. Add cubed chicken and toss to coat. Season with salt and pepper.

3. Place chicken in a single layer on a greased baking sheet and bake for 15 minutes until browned and 170 degrees in the middle. Cool completely.

4. In a small bowl mix mayonnaise, yogurt, and chicken broth and whisk until smooth. Add chicken, grapes, cranberries, nuts, celery, and apples to a large-lidded container.

5. Pour half a cup of the dressing over the top, seal the lid and shake to coat. Add the remaining dressing if necessary and shake again to coat.

6. Serve on a bed of bibb lettuce leaves. Makes 4 servings.

Seasoned Bean and Egg Salad

Serves 4

Ingredients

- 4 hard boiled eggs, peeled and sliced
- 2, 15 oz BPA-free cans three bean salad
- 1/2 small red onion, thinly sliced
- 3 tbsp extra virgin olive oil
- 2 tbsp white vinegar
- 1 tbsp fresh lemon juice
- 1/2 tsp garlic powder
- 1 tsp Dijon mustard

Instructions

1. In a medium bowl whisk together oil, vinegar, lemon juice, garlic powder, and mustard until well blended.

2. Season with salt and pepper.

3. Add canned 3 bean salad mix and toss well to coat.

4. Refrigerate for 15 minutes to allow flavors to mingle. Top with sliced boiled eggs. Serves 4.

Roasted Mushroom and Pepper Wraps

Serves 4

Ingredients

- 4 gluten-free tortillas or gluten-free pita bread
- 1 each red, green, and yellow bell peppers
- 1 medium onion, cut into quarters
- 2 large Portabella mushrooms, stem and gills removed
- 1/2 cup balsamic vinegar, divided
- 1 tsp honey (optional)
- 2 tbsp olive oil
- 1/2 tsp each dried oregano and garlic powder
- 1/4 tsp each cayenne, cumin, and paprika
- Salt and pepper to taste

Instructions

1. Preheat oven to 400 degrees F. Place peppers and onion on a rack on a baking sheet. Roast for 25 minutes. While peppers and onions are roasting, marinate Portabella mushrooms in ¼ cup balsamic vinegar and 2 tbsp olive oil. After 20 minutes turn the peppers and onions over, add Portabellas to the pan and roast another 20-25 minutes. Remove from oven and place peppers in a paper bag. Fold the top of the bag to close. Allow to cool in the paper bag. Once cooled you should be able to peel the skins off the peppers and remove the stems and seeds easily.

2. In a small saucepan reduce marinade and the remaining 1/4 cup of balsamic by 1/2. Check for taste; if the reduction is too bitter add up to 1 tsp honey to offset. Set aside glaze to cool. Slice peppers, Portabellas, and onion into thick strips. Mix oregano, garlic powder, cayenne, cumin, and paprika in a small bowl and sprinkle over the vegetables, tossing to mix seasoning well. Salt and pepper to taste. Divide vegetable mix into 4 equal portions and place in the middle of 4 tortillas or pita bread. Drizzle with up to 1 tbsp balsamic glaze. Roll. Serves 4.

Homemade Hummus

Serves 4

 ## Ingredients

- 1 15oz BPA-free can of chickpeas, drained
- 1 clove of garlic
- 1 tbsp fresh lemon juice
- 1/4 cup tahini
- Olive oil
- Salt

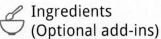 ## Ingredients (Optional add-ins)

- 1 tsp roasted garlic
- 1 tbsp Pine nuts
- 1 tbsp chopped sun dried tomatoes
- 1 tbsp roasted red peppers

Instructions

1. In a blender or food processor combine the first 4 ingredients and blend until a chunky paste forms.

2. Add 2 tbsp olive oil and blend until smooth, scraping the sides down at least once and pulsing again.

3. Season with salt and drizzle with olive oil.

4. Serve with gluten-free chips or carrot slices. Serves 4.

Savory Vegetable Soup

Simmer
1 to 1 1/2 hrs

Makes 16
1 cup servings

 Ingredients

- 2 cups organic vegetable juice such as R.W. Knudsen Organic Very Veggie Vegetable Juice Blend
- 1, 28 oz BPA-free can organic diced tomatoes
- 4 cups vegetable stock
- 1 tbsp olive oil
- 1 lb carrots, sliced
- 2 large onions, diced
- 4 celery ribs, chopped
- 1 red bell pepper, seeded and chopped
- 3 cloves minced garlic

- 2 cups each chopped cabbage, green beans, and peas
- 1 cup whole organic kernel corn
- 1, 15 oz can garbanzo beans, drained and rinsed
- 2 bay leaves
- 1 tbsp parsley
- 1 tsp each salt, dried marjoram, dried thyme, and dried basil
- 1/2 tsp pepper
- 1 cup grated parmesan cheese

Instructions

1. In a large stock pot, heat oil over medium heat. Add onion, bell pepper, celery, carrot, and bay leaves. Sauté for 5 minutes.

2. Add garlic and cook another 1-2 minutes. Add remaining ingredients, stir well and cover, bringing to a boil.

3. Reduce heat to low and simmer 1 to 1 1/2 hours until vegetables are tender.

4. Sprinkle 1 tbsp of parmesan cheese over each bowl of soup. Makes 16, 1 cup servings.

Spinach Salad
with Strawberries

Serves 4

 Ingredients

- 8 cups fresh spinach, washed and dried in salad spinner
- 1 small red onion, thinly sliced
- 1 lb strawberries, washed, hulled, and sliced
- 1 cup chopped spicy roasted pecans (recipe below)
- 1/3 cup feta crumbles
- Raspberry walnut vinaigrette dressing (recipe below)

Spicy Roasted Pecans:
- 1 lb pecan halves, about 4 cups
- 2 tsp cinnamon
- 1 tsp regular chili powder
- 1 tsp ancho chili powder
- 1 tsp cumin
- 1 tsp ground ginger
- 2 tsp salt
- 1/4 cup melted butter
- 1 tsp molasses
- 2 tsp liquid stevia

Raspberry Walnut Vinaigrette:
- 1/2 cup raspberry vinegar
- 2 tbsp walnut oil
- 2 tbsp extra virgin olive oil
- 1/4 cup walnuts
- 1/4 cup fresh raspberries
- 1/2 tsp garlic powder
- 2 tbsp liquid stevia
- 1/2 tsp salt
- 1/4 tsp fresh black pepper
- 1/4 tsp Dijon mustard

🍲 Instructions

Salad:

Mix spinach, onions, strawberries, spicy roasted pecans, and cheese crumbles in a large salad bowl. Dress with 1/4 cup dressing and toss well to coat.

Spicy Roasted Pecans:

Preheat oven to 400 degrees F. Roast pecans in a single layer on a baking pan lined with parchment paper for about 5 minutes until hot, shaking every other minute to move nuts around. In a medium bowl combine all other ingredients and mix well. Toss hot pecans with spice mix until well coated. Return to baking sheet and roast another 5 minutes, again shaking every few minutes until nuts are golden brown. Remove from hot pan immediately to prevent burning. Allow to cool.

Raspberry Walnut Vinaigrette:

Add all ingredients to a blender and blend at high speed until smooth.

Quinoa Tabouli Salad

Serves 4

 Ingredients

- 1 cup quinoa
- 2 cups vegetable broth
- 1 garlic clove, minced
- 1/4 cup each extra-virgin olive oil and avocado oil
- Freshly ground black pepper
- 1 large cucumber, peeled, seeded, and chunked
- 1 pint cherry tomatoes, halved
- 2/3 cup chopped flat-leaf parsley
- 1/2 cup chopped fresh mint
- 2 scallions, thinly sliced

Instructions

1. Bring vegetable broth and quinoa to a boil in a medium saucepan. Reduce heat to low, cover, and cook until almost all the liquid is absorbed, about 10 minutes. Turn off and keep tightly covered until remaining liquid is absorbed, about 5 minutes. Spread on a glass casserole dish to cool quickly.

2. In another bowl combine garlic, oil, and lemon juice. Whisk well.

3. In a large bowl add cooled quinoa, tomatoes, herbs, scallions, and cucumbers and mix together. Drizzle with half the dressing. Toss to coat. Taste, and adjust salt and pepper. Add additional dressing if desired. Serves 4.

Green Pea Soup

Serves 6

 Ingredients

- 2 tbsp coconut oil
- 1 small onion, minced
- 4 cups fresh or frozen peas
- 4 cups chicken stock
- 1 sprig mint
- Salt and pepper
- 4-6 tbsp full fat coconut milk
- 2 tsp chopped mint

Instructions

1. Sauté onion in coconut oil 4-5 minutes on low without browning.

2. Add 3 cups of peas, stock, coconut milk, salt, pepper, and mint. Cover and cook gently about 20 minutes.

3. Remove the mint sprig and move soup to a blender. Blend until smooth and return to the cooking vessel. Keep warm on lowest heat.

4. In a separate pot cook the remaining cup of peas in a little boiling, salted water.

5. Divide soup among 6 soup cups. Garnish with the whole cooked peas. Serves 6.

Quinoa and Black Bean Salad

Serves 4

We recommend using organic vegetables and fruits for all the recipes in this book, but never more so than with corn. Corn that's not organic is almost certainly genetically modified. The two things we can say with certainty about Jesus' diet is that he did not eat genetically modified (GMO) foods and he did not eat foods treated with pesticides or herbicides. To read more about the research on the adverse health effects of GMO-foods, pesticides, and herbicides, please read *The Disciples Diet* book.

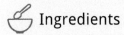 Ingredients

- 2 cups uncooked quinoa
- 4 cups vegetable stock
- 1, 15 oz BPA-free can black beans
- 1 small red onion, diced
- 1 Roma tomato, diced
- 1 small red bell pepper, diced
- 1 jalapeno, stemmed, seeded, and diced
- 1, 8 oz BPA-free can organic corn

- 1 avocado, diced
- 2 cloves of garlic, minced
- Juice of 2 limes
- 1/2 tsp salt
- 1/4 cup chopped cilantro

For the Dressing:
- 1/4 cup olive oil
- 1/4 cup fresh lime juice
- 2 tsp honey
- 1 clove garlic

🍴 Instructions

1. Cook quinoa in vegetable stock and garlic following package directions, about 20 minutes, until fluffy and liquid is absorbed.

2. Spread quinoa in a glass casserole dish to cool to avoid overcooking.

3. In a large bowl combine onion, bell pepper, jalapeno, black beans, corn, tomato, avocado, lime juice, and salt and stir well to combine.

4. In a blender add garlic clove and lime juice, set on liquify to incorporate the garlic.

5. Add olive oil and honey and pulse for a few seconds to combine.

6. Lightly dress the salad with 1/2 of the dressing and mix to combine.

7. Add cooled quinoa to the bowl of vegetables and fold together.

8. Garnish with plenty of fresh chopped cilantro.

9. Serve with the rest of the dressing on the side.

*Note: Can also be served warm

The Fatted Calf Soup

Serves 8

People in Jesus' time probably didn't eat a lot of beef. It was something saved for special occasions. We can conclude this from the parable Jesus told about the Prodigal Son. The father killed the fatted calf in honor of His son's return, indicating it was something to be saved for celebrations.

 Ingredients

Stock:

- 3 lbs grass fed beef shin
- 1 lb grass fed beef marrow bones
- 1 onion studded with 4 cloves
- 1 bay leaf
- 1/2 tsp crumbled dried thyme
- 1 cup crushed tomato
- 1 stalk celery
- 1/4 cup chopped parsley
- 2 tsp salt
- 10 cups water

Soup:

- 1 turnip, diced and peeled
- 1 large thinly sliced onion
- 3 peeled, sliced carrots
- 2 stalks sliced celery
- 2 cups tomatoes, peeled and chopped
- 1/4 cup chopped parsley
- 1/4 head of a medium cabbage
- 1/2 cup wild rice or brown rice

Instructions

Day One:

1. Roast beef shin and bones in a 400 degree F oven until browned.

2. Place in a large Dutch oven with remaining stock ingredients and bring to a boil. Skim if necessary.

3. Simmer 3 to 4 hours with the lid tilted slightly until the meat falls from the bones.

4. Strain stock and refrigerate, discarding vegetables.

5. Allow meat to cool, remove bones, fat, and gristle. Chop the meat and reserve for the soup.

Day Two:

1. Combine stock, meat, and soup ingredients in a large Dutch oven. Bring to a boil and cover.

2. Reduce heat to low and cook until vegetables and rice are tender, about 50 minutes. Serves 8.

Baba Ganoush

Serves 4

 Ingredients

- 1 medium eggplant
- 2 tbsp tahini
- 2 tbsp lemon juice
- 1 clove garlic, minced
- 1/4 teaspoon ground cumin
- Salt to taste
- 1 teaspoon olive oil
- Optional parsley for garnish

Instructions

1. Preheat oven to 400 degrees F.

2. Slice eggplant in half lengthwise and place on a baking sheet covered with parchment paper, skin side down. Bake until eggplant is very soft, about 30-40 minutes. Cool until eggplant can be handled.

3. Combine remaining ingredients in a medium bowl. Drain any juice from the eggplant, then scrape out the flesh like you would a baked potato, discarding the skin.

4. Mash ingredients together with a fork until well combined.

5. Allow to cool to room temperature before serving. Garnish with parsley if desired. Can be served with gluten-free pita bread or crackers or carrot sticks. Serves 4.

Broccoli Slaw
with Chickpeas

Serves 4

Like corn, soy is another ingredient that's usually genetically modified (GMO) if it's not organic. Jesus did not eat GMO food. If you decide to use the soy sauce for this recipe, be sure to buy organic. You can learn more about the research showing GMOs are harmful in *The Disciples Diet* book.

 Ingredients

- 1 bag pre-mixed broccoli slaw
- 1 can chickpeas, drained, rinsed and patted dry

Dressing:
- 1 tbsp sesame oil
- 2 tbsp extra virgin olive oil
- 2 tbsp liquid aminos or gluten-free organic soy sauce
- 2 tbsp balsamic vinegar
- 1/2 tsp garlic powder
- 2 tbsp minced ginger
- 1 tbsp honey
- 2 tbsp water

Instructions

1. Combine chickpeas and broccoli slaw in a large bowl.

2. Add all dressing ingredients in a jar with a screw top lid. Shake well to combine.

3. Dress with 1/2 the dressing and toss to coat. Add more dressing by the tsp to taste. Serves 4.

Chef Salad

Serves 4

We include avocadoes in some of the recipes in this book, even though they're a tropical fruit Jesus didn't eat. But they're nutritious, have a lot of potassium, and fit the low-glycemic requirement of most of the foods included in *The Disciples Diet*. Although the Chef Salad is thought to have originated in New York and wasn't a staple during Jesus' time, it is something healthy that you can whip up for lunch when you don't have a lot of time. The ingredients are all permissible on *The Disciples Diet*.

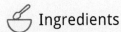 Ingredients

- 4 cups organic mixed salad greens
- 1 hardboiled egg, chopped
- 1 oz raw milk cheddar cheese, shredded
- 1 tbsp minced turkey bacon
- 1 oz each chopped turkey ham, boneless skinless chicken breast, and roast beef
- 4 cherry tomatoes, halved
- 6 - 8 thin slices of red onion
- 1/2 small cucumber, sliced
- 1/4 of an avocado, diced
- 2 tbsp dressing of choice

Instructions

1. Wash salad greens and remove excess moisture.

2. Toss with 2 tbsp salad dressing.

3. Arrange egg, avocado, and meat on top of the salad.

4. Sprinkle cheese, tomatoes, and cucumbers on top. Season with salt and pepper.

Chicken and Red Cabbage Slaw with Tahini Dressing

Serves 4

Tahini is made from ground sesame seeds. Sesame seeds are considered the oldest oilseed crop humans have produced. It was first domesticated well over 3,000 years ago, likely in India. However, there's evidence that people in Egypt were growing sesame seeds during and before Cleopatra's reign. Records and archeological evidence indicate sesame was also grown in Babylon and Turkey thousands of years ago. It can grow in areas where other crops can't and it has the highest oil content of any seed.

 Ingredients

- 3/4 pound boneless, skinless organic, free range chicken breast, grilled, cooled, and chopped
- 5 tablespoons extra-virgin olive oil
- 3 tablespoons fresh lemon juice
- 3 tsp minced garlic
- Salt and pepper to taste
- 1/2 head shredded red cabbage
- 1 small red onion, thinly sliced
- 1/3 cup tahini paste
- 1/2 cup each roughly chopped fresh mint, parsley, and cilantro leaves
- 1 tablespoon roasted sesame seeds

 Instructions

1. Massage chicken with 2 tbsp olive oil, 1 tbsp lemon juice, and 1 tsp minced garlic. Add cabbage, red onion, herbs, and half the sesame seeds.

2. In a separate bowl combine tahini, 2 tbsp lemon juice, and 2 tsp minced garlic.

3. Slowly whisk in 3 tbsp olive oil and enough water to make a thick dressing.

4. Season with salt and pepper. Toss dressing and salad together to coat. Sprinkle the remaining sesame seeds over the top.

Beef Stock

Serves 6

 Ingredients

- 4 to 5 cups clear jellied beef
- 2-3 small beets, cooked, peeled and grated
- 1-2 tsp onion juice Juice of ½ lemon
- 4-6 tbsp sour cream (optional)
- 1 lemon cut into quarters

Instructions

1. Place stock, onion juice, and beets into a large saucepan and heat on very low heat, covered for 30-40 minutes. Do not allow soup to boil.

2. Strain through 2 layers of cheesecloth. Add lemon juice, and adjust seasoning, adding salt if needed.

3. Reheat to just under a boil and serve with sour cream on the side. Serves 6.

Ginger Beef

Serves 4

 Ingredients

- 3 lbs grass-fed sirloin tip roast or London broil, fat trimmed off
- 1 cup onion, minced
- 3 cloves garlic, minced
- 2 tsp turmeric
- 2 tsp fresh grated ginger
- 1 tsp chili powder
- 1 tsp salt
- 8 tomatoes, peeled and roughly chopped
- 4 cups beef broth or bullion
- 1 red bell pepper, julienned
- 3 tbsp olive oil

Steamed Vegetables:
- 2 cups broccoli florets
- 2 cups cauliflower florets
- 1 cup slivered carrots
- 1 cup snow pea pods
- Liquid aminos

Instructions

Steamed Vegetables:

1. Steam for 5 minutes until vegetables are crisp tender. Season with liquid aminos using a mister.

Ginger Beef:

1. Combine onions, garlic, turmeric, ginger, chili powder, and salt in a large bowl and mix well.

2. Cut beef into 2-inch pieces. Toss with onion and garlic mix and refrigerate for 3 hours or up to overnight.

1. Heat oil in a large skillet. Stir fry beef until browned on all sides. Add to a greased casserole dish and add tomatoes, bullion, and skillet drippings. Bake for 2 hours in a 325-degree F oven about 2 hours until beef is tender. Serve with steamed brown rice and steamed vegetables. Garnish with red bell pepper strips.

Chickpea and Tomato Salad

Serves 4

Chickpeas were eaten regularly in Jesus' time. Tomatoes were not available in the Middle East back then, but they're loaded with lycopene and healthy for most people so we're including them in some recipes in this book.

 ## Ingredients

- 1, 15oz can chickpeas, drained and rinsed
- 2 pints multicolor cherry tomatoes, halved
- 2 tsp cumin
- 1/4 cup chopped fresh parsley
- 1/4 cup chopped fresh basil
- 1/4 cup olive oil, divided
- 1 tbsp red wine vinegar
- 1/2 tsp onion powder
- 1/2 tsp garlic powder
- 1/2 tsp Dijon mustard

Instructions

1. Preheat oven to 450 degrees F.

2. Toss chickpeas with 2 tbsp olive oil and place on a parchment-lined baking sheet. Bake about 10 minutes, shaking the pan every 2 minutes until chickpeas are golden brown. Removed from oven and sprinkle with cumin, shaking the pan to coat.

3. In a large mixing bowl add remaining 2 tbsp olive oil, vinegar, onion, and garlic powder and mustard. Whisk well to combine. Add tomatoes, parsley, and basil to the bowl. Pour chickpeas over the top and toss all ingredients well to coat. Season with salt and fresh cracked black pepper.

Chickpea Salad with Mustard Vinaigrette

Serves 4-8

 Ingredients

- 4 oz drained canned chick peas
- 1/2 cup each chopped celery, tomato, and cucumber
- 2 tbsp wine vinegar
- 1 tbsp lemon juice
- 1 tbsp parsley
- 2 tsp olive oil
- 1 clove minced garlic
- 1/4 tsp spicy brown mustard
- Pinch of salt, pepper and oregano

 Instructions

1. Combine all ingredients in a glass bowl. Cover and refrigerate at least an hour before serving.

Curried Quinoa Salad

Serves 4-8

Ingredients

- 1 cup quinoa
- 1/2 tsp salt
- 1 teaspoon yellow curry powder
- 1 cup water
- 1 cup vegetable or chicken stock
- 1 cup diced carrots

- 1 cup canned chickpeas, drained and rinsed
- 1 cup edamame beans
- 1/4 cup thinly sliced green onions

- 1/3 cup dried cranberries (fruit-juice sweetened)
- 1/2 cup slivered almonds
- 2 tablespoons chopped cilantro

Dressing:

- 1/4 cup plain grass fed yogurt or coconut yogurt
- 1/4 cup extra virgin olive oil
- 1 tsp apple cider vinegar

- 3/4 teaspoon mild yellow curry powder
- 1/4 tsp garam masala
- 1/4 tsp garlic powder

- 1/2 tsp paprika
- 1/4 tsp turmeric
- 1/2 tsp sea salt
- 1/4 tsp freshly ground black pepper

Instructions

1. Bring water, stock, salt, and 1 tsp curry powder to a boil. Add quinoa, cover and cook for 10 minutes. Add carrots, edamame beans, and chickpeas and cook until all the liquid is absorbed, about another 10 minutes. Spread in a glass casserole dish to quick cool.

2. In the meantime, whisk all dressing ingredients together in a small bowl. When quinoa is cool place in a mixing bowl and add green onions, cranberries and cilantro. Pour dressing over the top and toss lightly to coat.

Chilled Seafood Salad
In Lettuce Wraps

Serves 4

 Ingredients

- 3 tbsp butter
- 1 clove garlic, chopped
- 1 leek, cleaned and sliced
- 1 medium onion, chopped
- 1 1/2 cups each poached wild salmon and cod, chilled Salt & pepper
- 1/4 tsp tabasco
- 1 small head bibb lettuce
- 1 lemon, quartered

Instructions

1. Melt butter in a small skillet. Add garlic, leek, and onion, sauté until tender.

2. Chop onion mixture.

3. Flake fish and toss together gently.

4. Season with salt, pepper, and tabasco. Refrigerate until serving time.

5. Line plates with bibb lettuce, mound fish mix in the center of the plate, and garnish with lemon wedges. Serves 4.

Cream of Carrot Soup

Serves 6

Ingredients

- 1 1/2 cups sliced carrots
- 1 large onion, sliced
- 1/2 clove crushed garlic
- 2 tbsp brown rice
- 1 tbsp dried parsley
  Rind from 1/2 orange
- 4 cups chicken stock
- Juice of 1/2 orange
- 1/4 cup full fat coconut milk
- 1 tbsp Bob's Red mill egg replacer mixed with 4 tbsp water
- Salt and pepper
- 2 tbsp olive oil

Instructions

1. Heat olive oil in a Dutch oven.

2. Add vegetables, garlic, and rice. Cook on low heat for 5 minutes. Do not allow the vegetables to brown.

3. Add parsley, orange rind, stock, and seasonings. Bring to a boil then reduce heat to a simmer and cook for around 30 minutes until carrots are tender.

4. Move soup to a blender and process until smooth.

5. Return to the Dutch oven and add orange juice.

6. Mix coconut milk and egg replacer, temper with hot soup, then add gradually back to the pot, stirring constantly.

7. Reheat without allowing to boil. Serves 6.

Endive Salad with Lemon Mustard Vinaigrette

Serves 4-8

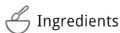 Ingredients

- 2 Belgian Endives
- 1 cup cherry tomatoes, halved
- 4 hard boiled eggs, cooled, peeled, and sliced
- Lemon mustard vinaigrette (recipe below)

Lemon Mustard Vinaigrette:

- 2 tbsp olive oil
- 1 tbsp white wine vinegar
- 1 tbsp fresh lemon juice
- 2 tsp Dijon mustard
- Pinch of granulated garlic or garlic powder
- Pinch of paprika

Instructions

Endive Salad:

1. Chop endive into bite-size pieces. Toss into a large salad bowl.

2. Add cherry tomatoes. Toss with lemon mustard vinaigrette.

3. Divide into 4 servings and garnish with hard boiled eggs cut into quarters.

Lemon Mustard Vinaigrette:

1. Add all ingredients to a small glass jar with a tight fitting lid. Shake well to combine.

2. Place in the refrigerator for at least 30 minutes.

3. Shake before serving.

Falafel Wraps with Tzatziki Sauce

Serves 4

 Ingredients

For the Tzatziki Sauce:
- 2 cups plain unsweetened Greek yogurt
- 2 cucumbers
- 3 cloves of garlic
- 2 tbsp chopped fresh dill
- 1 teaspoon olive oil
- 1/2 lemon, juiced
- Salt and pepper to taste

For the Falafel Balls:
- 1 cup dried chickpeas
- 1/2 small onion, chopped
- 2 garlic cloves
- 1 tsp cumin
- 1/2 tsp coriander
- 1/2 tsp salt
- 1/4 cup fresh parsley, chopped
- 1/4 tsp black pepper
- 1/8 tsp ground cardamom
- 2 teaspoons sesame seeds

For the Falafel Wrap:
- 4 gluten-free wraps
- 1 cup cherry tomatoes, halved
- 1 cup cucumber, quartered and sliced
- 1/2 cup red cabbage, grated
- 1/4 cup red onion, thinly sliced
- some shredded lettuce

⌂ Instructions

Tzatziki Sauce:
Peel and seed cucumber. Pulse in a food processor until well chopped. Line a colander with a lint-free towel and add cucumber, sprinkling with salt to draw out the excess moisture. Allow to sit at least an hour, then twist the cucumber in the towel tightly to remove all the water you can. Crush and mince garlic and add to food processor bowl with yogurt, cucumbers, dill, olive oil, and lemon juice. Pulse several times until ingredients are well combined. Pour into a small bowl and cover tightly. Place in the refrigerator for at least an hour to allow flavors to combine

Falafel Balls:
Soak the chickpeas overnight in cold water. The next day drain well and place on paper towel to remove the remaining exterior water. Add all ingredients to a food processor and pulse until roughly mashed. It should be a slightly chunky paste consistency. If the mixture is too moist or sticky at this stage, add a little bit of gluten-free flour, until the mixture holds together. Move to a bowl, cover with a lid or glass plate and allow to rest in the refrigerator for an hour. Once the falafel mixture has chilled, shape it into 12 small balls. Mist all over with an oil mister then arrange in a single layer in the basket of your preheated air fryer. Cook until browned at 375 degrees F for about 15 minutes.

Assembly:
Heat the wraps in a sprinkling of olive oil on a preheated skillet until soft (an iron skillet works well). Layer the tortilla with tomatoes, cucumber, cabbage, onion, and lettuce. Place 3 falafel balls in a line on top of the salad. Drizzle with tzatziki sauce.

Egg Salad Wraps

Serves 4

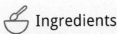 Ingredients

- 4 gluten-free tortilla wraps
- 6 eggs
- 1/4 cup plain unsweetened grass-fed yogurt
- 2 tbsp honey-sweetened mayonnaise
- 3/4 cup celery, chopped
- 1 tsp mustard
- Salt and pepper to taste
- 1 cup cherry tomatoes, halved
- 1 small bunch each arugula and watercress, washed and patted dry

Instructions

1. Boil eggs, cool, and peel. Coarsely chop eggs, stir in celery.

2. Mix mustard, yogurt, and mayonnaise together in a small bowl and mix the dressing into the egg and celery mixture.

3. Season to taste with salt and pepper.

4. Split egg filling into 4 portions and spread on a gluten-free tortilla staying half-inch away from the edges.

5. Add arugula, watercress, and tomatoes. Roll. Serves 4.

Dinner Entrees

Salmon with Pomegranate Salsa

Mediterranean Chicken

Serves 4

 Ingredients

- 4 boneless, skinless organic free-range chicken breasts
- 2 cloves minced garlic
- 1 tbsp dried oregano
- 1 tbsp dried thyme
- 1/2 cup dry white wine
- 1/2 cup chicken broth
- 1 cup red onion, finely chopped
- 1/4 cup sliced green olives
- 1 BPA-free can diced tomatoes
- 6 tbsp chopped fresh parsley
- 6 tbsp feta cheese
- Salt and pepper

Instructions

1. In skillet, sauté garlic and diced red onion in olive oil on low heat until soft.

2. Season chicken breasts on both sides with salt and pepper. Place chicken breasts into skillet with garlic and onions. Turn heat up to medium. Brown chicken on both sides.

3. Add the white wine and reduce by half. Add the chicken broth. Sprinkle with the oregano and thyme. Cover with a lid and cook for 20 minutes, turning the chicken over once. Make sure the chicken's internal temperature is 165 degrees.

4. Uncover and add the diced tomatoes and olives. Cover and cook for 5 minutes.

5. Remove from heat and stir in the parsley. Serve with brown rice and top with feta cheese. Serves 4.

Salmon with Pomegranate Salsa

Serves 4

Pomegranates are native to the Middle East and what was known as the Persian Empire during Jesus' time. This was an area that included Israel, Jordan, Syria, and Egypt. They're mentioned a number of times in the Bible. It's likely Jesus and His contemporaries ate the seeds from this red fruit.

 Ingredients

- 4, 6 oz wild salmon fillets (we recommend Vital Choice wild salmon, www.vitalchoice.com)
- 1/4 tsp sea salt
- 1/4 tsp pepper
- 2 tbsp olive oil
- Juice from 3 lemons

Pomegranate Salsa:
- 2 cups chopped heirloom tomatoes
- Seeds from 1 large pomegranate
- Half a green bell pepper chopped
- 1 red onion, chopped
- 10 mint leaves, chopped
- 1/2 cup fresh parsley, chopped
- Juice from 1 lime
- 1/2 cup feta cheese, crumbled
- Salt and pepper
- 1 tsp organic extra virgin olive oil

Instructions

1. Cover bottom of skillet with 2 tbsp olive oil. Add lemon juice. Place salmon in skillet. Sprinkle salt and pepper over the fish. Cook salmon on medium heat for about 20 minutes (10 minutes each side) until it's translucent in the center.

2. While it's cooking, assemble the salsa by combining all the salsa ingredients in a large bowl.

3. When the fish is done cooking, divide it on to four plates and top with the salsa. Serve with brown rice. Serves 4.

Steamed Salmon and Lemon Butter Sauce with Butternut Squash and Dates

Serves 4

Jesus ate a lot of fish. However, salmon wasn't available to Him. He mostly consumed tilapia, which was abundant in the Sea of Galilee. However, many of the recipes in this book include wild salmon because it's one of the healthiest fish available today. It has a high omega-3 content, which offsets any toxins that the fish picks up from today's modern polluted oceans. Plus, much of the wild salmon available today is from Alaska, where the ocean and river waters are less polluted.

 ## Ingredients

- 4, 6 oz salmon fillets (we recommend Vital Choice wild salmon, www.vitalchoice.com)
- 4 tbsp unsalted butter
- 3/4 tsp lemon juice
- 1/4 tsp sea salt
- 1/4 tsp pepper

For the Squash and Dates:
- 1 butternut squash
- 7 pitted dates
- 2 tbsp chopped fresh parsley
- Juice of 1 lemon
- 1 tsp cinnamon
- 2 tbsp olive oil
- 1/4 cup chopped pistachios or walnuts

🍳 Instructions

Butternut Squash:

1. Preheat oven to 350 degrees F.

2. Grease a 9 x 13 inch glass casserole dish with olive oil.

3. Dice the squash into 1 inch cubes and place in bowl.

4. Chop the dates into small pieces and add to the squash along with the fresh parsley, lemon juice, nuts, cinnamon, and olive oil. Stir this mixture to combine and place in the casserole dish.

5. Place in preheated oven and bake for 40 to 45 minutes or until the squash is tender.

Salmon:

1. Boil 1 inch of water in a large pot.

2. Place the salmon, skin side down, in a large steamer basket. Sprinkle with a 1/4 tsp salt and 1/4 tsp pepper.

3. Set the steamer basket into the pot over the boiling water and cover. Cook on medium high heat until the salmon is translucent in the center. About 5 minutes usually works for 1 inch fillets.

4. Add butter and lemon juice to a small saucepan and heat on low until the butter melts.

5. Arrange the salmon on plates and spoon the lemon butter sauce over the fish. Serve with the butternut squash casserole. Serves 4.

Salmon with Mustard Yogurt Sauce

Serves 4

We can presume that people in Jesus' time ate mustard due to the mentions in the bible of mustard seed. In Matthew 17:20, Jesus says, "For truly, I say to you, if you have faith like a grain of mustard seed, you will say to this mountain, 'Move from here to there,' and it will move, and nothing will be impossible for you." Even though Dijon mustard originated in France and was not part of Jesus' diet, it is one of the most flavorful mustards available. For that reason, we prefer to use it rather than a type of mustard that might be more similar to what people ate in Jesus' time.

 Ingredients

- 4, 6 oz salmon fillets (we recommend Vital Choice wild salmon, www.vitalchoice.com)
- 3 tbsp olive oil
- ½ tsp sea salt
- 1 cup unsweetened plain grass-fed yogurt or coconut yogurt
- 6 tbsp Dijon mustard
- 3 tbsp chopped shallots
- 2 tbsp butter

Instructions

1. Coat skillet with olive oil. Pour 1/4 cup water into pan. Place fish in pan and sprinkle with salt. Cook on medium-low heat until fish is translucent in the center.

2. In a medium-sized pot, sauté the shallots until soft. Add the yogurt and Dijon mustard and stir just until it's heated through (don't let it boil).

3. Spoon the sauce over the salmon. Serve this over brown rice pasta or with brown rice.

Sweet Potato Rosemary Soup

Serves 4

Ingredients

- 4 large sweet potatoes or yams
- 5 cups chicken broth
- 5 tbsp fresh rosemary
- 1 small white onion
- 1 tbsp fresh grated ginger

Instructions

1. Peel sweet potatoes and chop into 2-inch pieces. Place in pot. Pour chicken broth over sweet potatoes. Cook on medium-high heat until sweet potatoes are soft, about 25 minutes. Cool for ten minutes.

2. Remove rosemary from stem and chop into small pieces.

3. Cut onion into small pieces. Place onion into a skillet and sauté until onion is soft. Add rosemary and cook for 1 minute more. Remove from heat.

4. Puree slightly cooled sweet potatoes and chicken broth in a blender.

5. Pour back into pot. Add onions and rosemary to the pot and then the ginger. Salt and pepper to taste.

6. Heat soup in pot for 3 more minutes on medium or until steaming hot. Serves 4.

Kofte in Tomato Sauce

Bake
30-40 min.

Serves 4

Kofte—otherwise known as meatballs—are a traditional Turkish dish. However, people in Israel, Palestine, and Jordan and other areas have their own versions of kofte. Neither Jesus nor His disciples ate tomatoes. The earliest known consumption of tomatoes was among the Aztecs in 700 A.D. They likely originated in the Americas. Even though Jesus and His contemporaries did not eat tomatoes, we're including them in some recipes because their high lycopene content makes them a healthy choice for most people. However, some people are intolerant to them. We recommend you read more about food intolerance testing in *The Disciples' Diet* book.

 Ingredients

- 1/2 cup cider or dry white wine
- 2 slices stale gluten free bread
- 1 lb ground lamb
- 1 large onion, grated
- 1 tbsp parsley
- 1 tsp thyme
- 1 tsp lemon rind
- 2 tsp paprika
- Salt
- 2 eggs, beaten
- 2-3 tbsp seasoned rice flour
- 2 tbsp olive oil
- 1 cup unsweetened grass fed or coconut yogurt

Tomato Sauce:
- 1 tbsp olive oil
- 1 medium onion, thinly sliced
- 1 clove garlic, crushed
- 1 cup peeled, chopped tomato
- 1 tbsp parsley
- 1 tsp basil
- Salt and pepper
- 1 tsp paprika
- Cider from soaked bread (see instructions)

....   🍳   ....

🍳 Instructions

Tomato Sauce:

1. Cook onion and garlic in olive oil for 5 minutes or until onion is translucent.
2. Add remaining ingredients and heat to boiling.

Kofte:

1. Pour cider or wine over bread and soak for 5 minutes.
2. In a large bowl combine meat, onion, parsley, thyme, lemon rind, paprika, and salt.
3. Squeeze cider out of bread and crumble bread over meat mixture. Beat mix by hand, adding eggs one at a time. Beat for 7 to 10 minutes to give meatballs their light texture. Wet hands and roll meat into 1-inch balls then dredge in seasoned flour.
4. Heat olive oil in a large skillet and brown meatballs all over. Move meatballs to an ovenproof dish and pour tomato sauce over the top.
5. Bake at 350 degrees for 30-40 minutes. Serve with yogurt spooned on top. Garnish with parsley. Serve with squash noodles (see recipe under side dishes) or buy squash noodles at Whole Foods Market. Serves 4.

Spaghetti Squash with Chicken, Asparagus, and Marinated Artichokes

Cook
45-60 min.

Bake
45 min.

Serves 4

 Ingredients

- 1 spaghetti squash
- 4 chicken thighs
- Juice of two lemons
- 12 sticks asparagus
- 1 package fresh mushrooms
- 2, 6.5 oz. jars of marinated artichokes (usually difficult to find organic)
- 8 tbsp olive oil
- 8 tbsp parmesan cheese

Instructions

1. Place 4 tablespoons of the olive oil with the juice of two lemons into a large bowl. Place the chicken in the bowl and turn to coat. Place chicken in a skillet with the olive oil and lemon mixture. Add a half cup water. Heat on medium. Turn the chicken after 20 minutes. Cook for 45 minutes to an hour until the chicken is ready. Place the chicken on a plate, let cool for 15 minutes, then take the meat off of the bones, place into a bowl and set aside.

2. While the chicken is cooking, slice spaghetti squash in half lengthwise. Scoop out the seeds and discard. Place in a 9 x 13 inch glass baking dish. Place about an inch of water in the bottom of the dish. Bake in a preheated 350 degree oven for 45 minutes. Set aside to cool for 15 minutes.

3. Chop and clean asparagus and mushrooms. Place in a skillet with the remaining 4 tablespoons of the olive oil. Sauté on medium-low heat until soft. Add artichokes and heat just until warmed. Add chicken. Warm for another minute then remove from heat.

4. With a fork, remove the insides of the spaghetti squash into a medium to large bowl, depending upon the size of the squash.

5. Divide the spaghetti squash onto four plates. Top each plate with the artichoke-asparagus-chicken mixture. Sprinkle parmesan cheese over the plates. Serves 4

Roasted Apricot Salmon

Serves 4

 Ingredients

- 4, 6 oz wild salmon filets (we recommend Vital Choice wild salmon, www.vitalchoice.com)
- 1/2 cup unsweetened apricot preserves (or fruit juice sweetened)
- 1/4 tsp paprika
- 2 tbsp sesame oil
- 1/4 tsp garlic powder
- 3 tbsp finely chopped onion

Instructions

1. In a small bowl, whisk together the apricot preserves, paprika, sesame oil, garlic powder, and onion.

2. Place parchment paper on a cookie sheet. Place salmon on top of the parchment paper.

3. Spread 1/4 of the apricot mixture on top of each filet.

4. Roast in a 350-degree oven for about 20 minutes or until the salmon starts to flake. Serve over brown rice. Serves 4.

Balsamic Lamb Chops

Serves 2

Jesus very likely didn't have meat very often. When He did eat meat it was probably lamb, although the fatted calf mention in the Prodigal Son parable indicates cow meat was served on special occasions. This lamb chop recipe is a great choice for when you want a break from fish.

Ingredients

- 4 lamb chops
- 1 tsp dried rosemary
- 1/2 tsp dried thyme
- 1/4 tsp dried sage
- 1 tbsp olive oil
- 1/4 cup minced sweet onion
- 1/3 cup balsamic vinegar
- 3/4 cup chicken broth
- 1 tbsp butter
- Salt and pepper to taste

Instructions

1. In a medium bowl, combine the rosemary, thyme, sage, salt, and pepper. Rub this mixture on both sides of the lamb chops. Let the chops sit in the bowl for a half hour. Place olive oil in skillet and turn to medium-high heat. Cook lamb in the skillet for about 3 ½ minutes on each side if you like them medium rare, longer if you prefer them more done. Remove from heat onto a platter and set aside. Add the onion to the skillet and cook until browned. Add the vinegar, then the chicken broth. Cook over medium-high heat for 5 minutes, stirring constantly, until the mixture is reduced by half. Remove from heat. Stir in the butter and pour over the lamb chops.

2. Serve with brown rice and a vegetable. Serves 2.

Salmon and Pasta with Lemon Butter Parsley Sauce

Serves 4

 Ingredients

- 4, 6 oz wild salmon filets (we recommend Vital Choice wild salmon, www.vitalchoice.com)
- 4 tbsp butter
- Juice of 4 lemons
- 4 tbsp chopped parsley
- 1 tbsp grated lemon rind
- 1 package brown rice pasta
- 1/4 tsp salt and pepper

Instructions

1. Place parchment paper on a cookie sheet. Place salmon filets on top of the parchment paper. Sprinkle with salt and pepper. Roast for about 20 minutes in a 350-degree oven until the fish begins to flake.

2. Meanwhile, boil pasta.

3. While fish and pasta are cooking, in a medium saucepan, melt butter with the lemon juice, stirring frequently. When melted, add parsley and stir. Cook for two more minutes and remove from stove.

4. Place pasta on a plate, put salmon on top of the pasta, and spoon the lemon-butter sauce over the fish and pasta. Serves 4.

Mediterranean Fish Stew

Serves 8

 Ingredients

- 2 medium onions, chopped
- 2 leeks, chopped
- 2 carrots, chopped
- 4 cloves of garlic, crushed
- 1/2 hot banana pepper, seeded and chopped fine
- 2 1/2 lbs mixed firm, meaty, wild fish such as cod, snapper, flounder, halibut, perch, or mullet, boned and cut into large chunks
- 4 tomatoes, peeled and chopped
- 1 bay leaf
- 1 tbsp chopped fennel
- Pinch of saffron
- 1 sprig thyme
- 4 stalks of parsley, chopped
- 3 cups fish stock
- 1 tsp lemon juice
- 1 cup white wine
- Salt and pepper
- 2 tbsp olive oil

Instructions

1. Heat oil in a large pan. Add onions, pepper, leeks, carrots, and garlic. Cook slowly until onions are translucent, stirring often.

2. Add tomatoes, bay leaf, fennel, saffron, thyme, and parsley then cook about 10 minutes.

3. Add fish stock, salt, and pepper. Cover and cook 30 minutes.

4. Add fish and bring soup to a boil until fish is almost cooked through, about 7 minutes.

5. Add wine and lemon juice, bring back to a boil another 2 minutes. Re-season if necessary.

6. Divide fish between 8 bowls and spoon broth over fish. Serves 8.

Stuffed Baked Sweet Potato

Serves 4

 Ingredients

- 1 1/2 lbs free range, organic chicken breast and thighs
- 1/2 yellow onion
- 4 sweet potatoes or yams
- 1 package whole mushrooms
- 1 bunch fresh spinach
- 3 tbsp Dijon mustard
- 1/4 cup unsweetened grass-fed yogurt or coconut yogurt
- 8 tbsp olive oil
- 4 tbsp parmesan cheese
- 1/2 tsp sea salt
- 4 tbsp chopped green onions or chives

 Instructions

1. Bake the sweet potatoes in an oven at 375 degrees for 50 minutes to 1 hour depending on size. Large potatoes may need a little longer. While the potatoes are cooking, place 4 tbsp olive oil in a pot. Put the chicken in the pot, cover with water, add salt, and let cook for an hour. Meanwhile, wash and chop the spinach and set aside. Coat skillet with 4 tablespoons olive oil. Place mushrooms and onions in the skillet and sauté over medium heat until soft. Add the chopped spinach and cook for about 5 minutes longer.

2. Drain the chicken, reserving the stock for future soup recipes. When the potatoes are done cooking, let them sit for about 10 minutes while you chop the chicken into small pieces. Cut the sweet potatoes in half and scoop out the innards into a bowl. Place the skins on a parchment-covered baking sheet. Add the chopped chicken and the sautéed mushrooms, onion, and spinach to the sweet potatoes in the bowl. Add the yogurt and Dijon mustard and mix. Spoon the mixture back into the potato skins. Place them back into a 325-degree oven and let warm up for about 15 minutes. Sprinkle each potato with 1 tablespoon parmesan cheese and 1 tablespoon green onions or chives.

Lemon Dill Cod

Bake
30 min.

Serves 2

 Ingredients

- 1 lb wild cod fish
- 1 tbsp chopped parsley
- 1 tbsp lemon juice
- 3/4 tsp seasoned salt
- 1 tbsp olive oil, plus more for brushing
- 3 sprigs of fresh dill
- 1 clove crushed garlic
- 2 tbsp white wine
- 1 lemon, sliced 2 cloves garlic
- Juice of 1/2 lemon

Instructions

1. Grease a baking dish with olive oil. Arrange fish in the baking dish and brush with a bit more olive oil. Sprinkle fish with crushed garlic and parsley then arrange dill over the fish. Place lemon slices on top then pour wine over all.

2. Bake at 350 degrees until fish is done and flakes easily, about 30 minutes.

Single Skillet Garden "Noodle" Dinner

Cook
5-10 min.

Serves 6

 Ingredients

- 4 large carrots
- 4 medium zucchini
- 4 medium yellow squash
- 1 cup canned chickpeas
- 1 pint cherry tomatoes, halved
- 1 thinly sliced red bell pepper
- 1 thinly sliced small red onion
- 1 recipe basil walnut pesto (below)
- 1 tbsp olive oil

Walnut Basil Pesto:

- In a blender or food processor add:
- 1 cup packed fresh basil leaves
- 1/3 cup chopped walnuts
- 1/4 cup freshly grated parmesan cheese
- 2 cloves garlic
- Juice of 1/2 lemon

🍳 Instructions

Garden "Noodle" Dinner:

Spiralize carrot, zucchini, and yellow squash to make "noodles" and place into separate bowls. This can be done using a spiralizer machine or a julienne peeler. See the recipe for Squash Noodles in the side dish section of this cookbook. Your local Whole Foods Market may also sell zucchini and yellow squash noodles in the vegetable section. Thinly slice bell pepper and onion. Cut cherry tomatoes in half. Prepare pesto (see recipe below) and set aside for flavors to combine while preparing the rest of the dish. In a large, deep skillet heat olive oil over medium heat. Add peppers, onions, chickpeas, and carrots and sauté for 5 minutes. Add zucchini and yellow squash noodles and cook just long enough to heat through. Add pesto and tomatoes and toss well to combine. Serve immediately. Makes 6 servings.

Walnut Basil Pesto:

Pulse ingredients until well chopped. Drizzle in 1/4 cup of extra virgin olive oil while continuing to process until incorporated. Scrape down sides and pulse again to combine.

Skillet Pasta

Serves 6

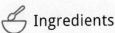 Ingredients

- 1, 12 oz box gluten-free pasta
- 2, 6 oz BPA-free cans marinated artichoke hearts
- 1 small jar roasted red peppers
- 1 cup large green olives, halved
- 1 pint cherry tomatoes, halved
- 1/4 cup Kalamata olives, chopped
- 1, 8oz package turkey salami (Zoe's Meats is a good brand)
- 2 cloves of garlic, crushed and minced
- 2 tbsp balsamic vinegar
- 1/4 cup olive oil

Instructions

1. Cook pasta according to package directions, drain, and hold in colander.

2. Return the pasta pan to the heat, and add all remaining ingredients to the pot. Sauté until heated through.

3. Add pasta back to the pot and toss well to combine. Continue to sauté to reheat pasta. Serves 6.

Poached Fish with Avocado Sauce

Serves 4

 Ingredients

- 2 lbs frozen wild flounder fillets, thawed, drained and patted dry 1 thin sliced onion
- 2 thin sliced lemons 1 tsp salt 1 bay leaf 1/2 tsp black pepper 3 cups fish stock
- 1 lemon, cut in half

Avocado Sauce:
- 2 avocadoes, mashed
- 1/2 cup unsweetened grass fed yogurt or coconut yogurt
- 2 tbsp lemon juice
- 1/2 small onion, grated

 Instructions

1. In a large Dutch oven, bring onion, lemon, salt, bay leaf, pepper, and stock to a boil.

2. Add fish and reduce to a simmer. Poach for 8-10 minutes or until the fish turns opaque and flakes easily.

3. Remove fish to an ice-filled baking dish to quick cool.

4. As soon as the fish is cooled transfer to an airtight container and place in the refrigerator for at least 2 hours.

5. When fish is completely chilled, assemble avocado sauce by mixing all ingredients well in a small bowl.

6. To serve spoon sauce over fish. Garnish with lemon wedges.

Balsamic Glazed Salmon

Serves 4

 Ingredients

- 4, 6oz wild salmon filets (we recommend Vital Choice wild salmon, www.vitalchoice.com)
- 1/2 cup balsamic vinegar
- 1/4 cup white wine
- 2 tbsp honey
- 1 tbsp Dijon mustard
- 1/8 tsp garlic powder
- 2 tsp olive oil
- Salt and pepper

Instructions

1. Allow fish to start to come to room temperature while preparing glaze.

2. In a medium saucepan combine vinegar, wine, honey, mustard, and garlic powder and whisk to combine. Bring to a boil then reduce heat and simmer until sauce has thickened and is reduced to about 1/3 cup, about 10-15 minutes.

3. Season salmon on both sides with salt and pepper. Mist olive oil in a large skillet over medium high heat. Cook fillets for 3-4 minutes, turn and cook 2-3 minutes longer or until salmon has cooked through. Serve hot, drizzled with glaze.

Fish Cakes

Serves 4

 Ingredients

- 1 lb pollock
- 1/2 cup canned French cut green beans in a BPA-free can
- 2 tbsp red curry paste
- 1/4 cup minced green onion
- 1/4 cup gluten-free flour
- 1 tsp fish sauce
- 1/2 tsp lemon zest

Instructions

1. Rinse fish and pat dry. Cut into chunks and place in the bowl of your food processor. Add remaining ingredients and pulse in the food processor until well combined. You should be able to easily form the mix into a ball. If the mix is too wet add additional flour by the teaspoon until corrected. Line a small baking sheet with parchment. Form paste into 12 balls, flattening slightly. Balls should be no more than 3/4-inch thick. Refrigerate for 10-15 minutes to firm up.

2. Preheat your air fryer for 10 minutes. Remove fish cakes from refrigerator and mist with olive oil. Arrange cakes in the basket in a single layer and air fry until golden brown, about 10-15 minutes. You can also cook in a frying pan on the stove top in a few tablespoons of olive oil.

Skillet Chicken Parmesan with Zucchini "Noodles"

Cook
60-90 min.

Serves 6

 Ingredients

- 3 chicken breasts, cut into 1/2" slices
- 2 tbsp organic, unsweetened Italian dressing
- 6 tbsp Parmesan cheese, grated

- 6 cups spiralized zucchini noodles, about 4 medium zucchini
- 6 tbsp mozzarella cheese, shredded

For the Marinara:

- 1 tbsp olive oil
- 1/2 of a large sweet onion, finely diced
- 8 large tomatoes, peeled, seeded, and chunked
- 6 cloves garlic, minced
- 1 bay leaf
- 1/2 cup red wine

- 1 tsp oregano
- 1 tsp marjoram
- 2 tsp basil
- 1 tsp salt
- 1/4 tsp fennel seed
- 1/4 tsp crushed red pepper
- 1 tbsp balsamic vinegar
- 1 tbsp honey (optional)

⟡ Instructions

1. Place chicken in a shallow glass dish and pour Italian dressing over the top. Toss to coat, cover, and refrigerate 1 hour while you're making the sauce. In a large saucepan over medium heat add olive oil, onion, garlic, bay leaf, and sauté about 7 minutes until onion is translucent, being careful not to allow vegetables to brown. Add tomatoes and bring to a boil. Reduce heat to low, cover, and simmer about 30 minutes, stirring occasionally. Stir in herbs, spices, and wine. Simmer another 30 minutes. Sir in balsamic vinegar. Check for flavor. If sauce is too bitter stir in honey and cook another 5 minutes.

2. Spiralize zucchini and spread out over a clean kitchen towel. To spiralize, use a spiralizer machine or a julienne peeler. Your local Whole Foods Market may also sell zucchini and yellow squash noodles in the vegetable section. Sprinkle with 1/2 tsp salt to draw out the moisture. Heat a large, deep skillet over medium heat. Spray with olive oil cooking spray. Add chicken in a single layer and sauté until cooked through. Add chicken to marinara sauce and keep at a simmer.

3. Add zucchini noodles to the skillet, using pan juices to sauté the zucchini. Cook for 2-3 minutes until noodles are hot and beginning to become tender.

4. To serve, place 1 cup noodles per plate, top with chicken in marinara, and sprinkle with 1 tbsp of each cheese. Serves 6.

Bandit Style Leg of Lamb

Bake
3 hrs.

Serves 4

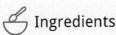 Ingredients

- 1, 4-5 lb leg of lamb that has been boned, rolled, and tied
- 2 cloves garlic, slivered
- Salt and pepper
- 2 tbsp butter
- 3 feet heavy duty aluminum foil
- 2 feet parchment paper
- 2 lbs pearl onions that have been peeled and parboiled
- 2 tbsp parsley
- 1 tsp dill
- 1/2 cup white wine
- 2 tbsp olive oil
- Juice of 1 lemon

Instructions

1. Cut slits in the fat on the outside of the lamb, insert garlic slivers. Brown all sides of the lamb in butter.

2. Place parchment paper on top of aluminum foil. Then place the lamb in the middle of the parchment paper. Add onions to skillet and cook until brown.

3. Add parsley and dill, spoon mix around lamb. Pour wine, oil, and lemon juice over lamb.

4. Fold foil and parchment paper tightly around lamb and place in a baking dish. Bake at 375 degrees for 3 hours.

Slow Cooker Pot Roast

Serves 8-10

Ingredients

- 2-3 lbs medium grass fed chuck roast
- 3-4 large onions
- 3 lbs carrots, washed and cut into 3-inch pieces
- 4 cups rutabaga, peeled, washed, and cut into 1-inch cubes
- 1, 8 oz package button mushrooms, cleaned, and stemmed
- 1 tbsp minced garlic
- 1 tbsp Worcestershire sauce
- 1/2 cup red wine

Instructions

1. The night before you plan to serve, spray the insert of a large slow cooker with olive oil cooking spray. Peel onions and slice into 1/4-inch slices. Line the bottom of the slow cooker with onions, place meat on top of the onions, and cut large slits in it. Push some garlic and slices of onion into the slits. Sprinkle Worcestershire sauce over the meat. Pour in red wine. Arrange remaining slices of onion around the sides of the slow cooker like an onion case around the roast. Cook on low overnight.

2. In the morning raise the meat and slide carrots and rutabaga underneath, then set the meat back down on top of it and tuck mushrooms in around the sides.

3. Cook on low 8 hours or until vegetables are tender. Serves 8-10.

Black Bean Soup

Serves 8

 Ingredients

- 1 1/2 cups dried beans
- 1 smoked turkey leg
- 6 cups water
- 2 medium onions sliced 4 stalks sliced celery
- 3 carrots sliced
- 1 bouquet garni (1 bay leaf, 5 sprigs parsley, 1 sprig thyme, 2 cloves wrapped in a cheesecloth pouch tied with butcher's twine)
- 1/2 tsp mustard powder
- Pinch of cayenne
- Chicken stock
- 2 hard boiled eggs
- 4-6 slices of lemon

Instructions

1. Wash beans thoroughly in cold running water. Place beans in 2-quart container, add water to cover, and soak overnight.

2. Drain. In a large Dutch oven add water, beans, and turkey leg, cover, and cook on low for 2 hours.

3. Add onion, carrot, celery, herb packet, mustard powder, and cayenne. Cover and cook an additional 1 to 1 1/2 hours until beans are tender.

4. Remove turkey leg and herb packet. Pour soup into a blender and process until smooth. Return to pan and check texture. If the soup is too thick add stock until desired consistency is reached. Check seasoning and add salt and pepper to taste.

5. Reheat to just under boiling. Garnish with sliced hard boiled eggs and lemon slices.

Chicken and Capers

Serves 2

Capers come from the caper bush (*Capparis spinosa* or *Capparis inermis*), which is native to Mediterranean countries such as Greece. The immature flower buds of the caper bush are what we call capers. Native wild capers have been incorporated into cuisine for centuries. When the Apostle Paul arrived in Greece to preach the Holy Gospel, it's likely that he ate dishes flavored with capers.

 Ingredients

- 1 8 oz boneless, skinless, organic, free range chicken breast, butterflied into 2 portions
- 1/4 cup thin-sliced celery
- 1/4 cup thin-sliced onion
- 1/2 cup seeded, chopped tomato
- 1 tbsp capers
- 1/3 cup dry white wine
- 2 tsp olive oil

Instructions

1. Add 1 tsp olive oil to skillet, heat until it shimmers, and add celery, onion, and garlic. Sauté, stirring constantly until vegetables are tender.

2. Add tomatoes and capers and continue cooking until tomatoes start to soften, about another 5 minutes.

3. Move vegetables to the side and pour in the other tsp of oil. Add chicken and brown on both sides. Add white wine and stir all ingredients together.

4. Cook until some of the liquid evaporates. Serves 2.

Fish Steaks

Serves 4-6

 Ingredients

- 6, 8 oz fillets of any firm, flaky white wild fish such as cod or sea bass. Avoid farm-raised fish.
- Salt and pepper
- 6 small lemons
- 6 tsp olive oil
- 6 tbsp dry white wine
- 1 clove garlic, crushed
- 2 tbsp chopped parsley

Instructions

1. Season fish with salt and pepper. Peel lemons, remove all white pith. Cut into thin slices. Cut 6 squares of foil and 6 squares of parchment paper double the size of the fish steaks.

2. Place the parchment paper on top of the foil to keep the aluminum away from the food. Arrange half of the lemon slices down the center of each foil-parchment square.

3. Place a fish steak on top and brush each with a teaspoon of olive oil and spoon 1 tbsp of wine over the top.

4. Place the rest of the lemon slices on top and sprinkle with parsley. Fold foil neatly to seal the packages.

5. Place on a baking sheet and bake at 375 degrees or steam in a bamboo steamer for 20 minutes.

Cod with Yogurt Herb Sauce

Serves 8-10

 Ingredients

- 1 1/2 lbs wild cod fillets
- 2 tbsp lemon juice
- 1 tbsp olive oil
- Salt and pepper
- Herb sauce
- 1/2 cup unsweetened coconut yogurt
- 1 tbsp parsley
- 1 tbsp chives
- 1 tsp dill
- 1/2 tsp tarragon
- 1/2 tsp chervil

Instructions

1. Preheat oven to 350 degrees. Lightly oil a baking dish with 1 tbsp olive oil.

2. Place fillets in dish and sprinkle lemon juice over the top. Salt and pepper to taste.

3. Bake uncovered in a 350 degree oven for about 20 minutes.

4. In a saucepan, combine herb sauce ingredients and heat through. Do not allow to come to a boil. To serve, top fish with sauce.

Garlic Chicken and Brown Rice

Bake
25 min.

Serves 4-6

 Ingredients

- 2 large organic, free-range chicken breasts, chopped into 1/2-inch cubes
- 1/4 cup roasted garlic, about 12 cloves
- 4 cups steamed brown rice
- 4 medium carrots, diced
- 1 small onion, diced
- 1 cup chopped red bell pepper
- 1 cup chopped water chestnuts
- 1 cup organic edamame
- 1/2 tsp rubbed sage
- 1/2 tsp rosemary
- 1/2 tsp basil
- 2 tbsp olive oil
- 1/2 cup chicken stock

Instructions

1. Preheat oven to 350 degrees. In a large skillet heat olive oil over medium heat. Sauté chicken until browned. Add onion, carrot, and bell pepper, and cook for 5 minutes.

2. Grease a medium baking dish.

3. In a large bowl mix rice, water chestnuts, edamame, and the contents of the skillet. Return the skillet to the stove, heat, and add chicken stock and roasted garlic.

4. Mash the garlic cloves with a fork and mix with the chicken stock to create a sauce. Add sage, rosemary, and basil and stir to combine.

5. Pour over the rest of the ingredients and mix thoroughly to combine.

6. Pour into the baking dish and bake for 25 minutes.

Side Dishes and Sauces

Creamy Cilantro Lime Slaw

Broccoli with Cashews and Lemon

Serves 4

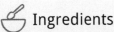 Ingredients

- 2 heads broccoli
- 1/2 cup olive oil
- Juice of two lemons
- 1/4 tsp lemon zest
- 1/8 tsp sea salt
- 1/8 tsp black pepper
- 1/2 cup cashews
- 1 medium minced garlic clove
- 1 medium sweet onion

 Instructions

1. Steam the broccoli for about 5 minutes until it first becomes tender.

2. Heat the olive oil and lemon juice in a large skillet or wok.

3. Add the broccoli, cashews, lemon zest, salt, pepper, garlic, and onion.

4. Sauté until the mixture begins to turn brown. Serves 4.

Squash Noodles

Serves 4

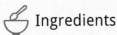 Ingredients

- 3 medium zucchini
- 3 medium yellow squash
- Salt and pepper

Instructions

1. Wash vegetables and trim off stem end and blossom end. Using a spiralizer cut all vegetables into long noddle shapes. Blanch in boiling water 1-2 minutes. Drain well and serve with a drizzle of olive oil and sprinkle of herbs of your choice.

Vegetable Cakes

Serves 4

 Ingredients

- 2 Tbsp olive oil
- 1 small yellow onion
- 2 cloves garlic, minced
- 3 cups fresh spinach
- 1 large parsnip
- 1 tsp dried oregano
- 1/4 cup sun dried tomatoes
- 1/4 cup kalamata olives
- 1/4 cup artichoke hearts
- 2 large eggs
- 1/4 cup almond flour
- 1/2 tsp sea salt
- 1/4 tsp black pepper

Instructions

1. Prepare the vegetables, keeping each separate. Finely dice the onion, artichokes, olives, and sun dried tomatoes. Mince the garlic. Heat 1 tbsp of oil over medium heat.

2. Sauté onion until soft, add garlic, and cook 1 minute more.

3. Add spinach and cook until wilted, then remove from the heat and pour into a large bowl.

4. Add the rest of the ingredients and stir to combine.

5. Divide into quarters and form into cakes.

6. Heat remaining 1 tablespoon olive oil in the skillet until it shimmers.

7. Fry the cakes for 5-7 minutes per side until brown and crispy.

Mixed Steamed Greens

Serves 4

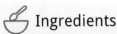 Ingredients

- 2 cups each packed kale, turnip greens, mustard greens, collard greens
- 2 cups water

Instructions

1. Place water in the bottom of a large pot. Place steamer insert in the bottom and fold out. Add greens. Cover tightly and steam over medium heat until greens are done to your desired level of tenderness. Five minutes for crisp tender, up to 15 minutes for soft. Serves 4.

Sautéed Asparagus

Serves 4

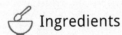 Ingredients

- 1 lb asparagus, washed, trimmed, and snapped or cut into 3-inch pieces
- 1 tbsp olive oil
- 1 clove garlic, minced
- Salt and pepper

Instructions

1. In a large skillet, sauté garlic in olive oil over medium heat for a minute. Add asparagus pieces. Cook, stirring frequently until crisp tender, about 5 minutes. Season with salt and pepper to taste.

Mixed Baked Squash and Sweet Potatoes

Serves 4

Ingredients

- 2 large sweet potatoes, peeled and cubed
- 2 cups acorn squash, peeled and cubed
- 1/2 tsp each parsley, sage, rosemary, thyme, onion powder, and garlic powder
- 1 tsp salt
- 1/4 tsp fresh cracked black pepper
- 2 tbsp olive oil

Instructions

1. Preheat oven to 375 degrees.
2. In a large mixing bowl, mix olive oil, herbs and spices, and salt and pepper. Add sweet potatoes and squash. Toss well to coat.
3. Roast in a 9 x 13-inch glass casserole pan for 1 hour to 90 minutes, depending on the size of the cubes, stirring every 30 minutes.

Steamed Brussels Sprouts

Serves 4

 Ingredients

- 1 lb Brussels sprouts, fresh or frozen
- 1 tbsp butter
- Salt and pepper to taste

Instructions

1. Steam brussels sprouts until crisp tender, about 6-8 minutes for fresh or 12 minutes for frozen. Toss with 1 tbsp of butter. Season with salt and pepper to taste.

Mashed Celeriac

Serves 4

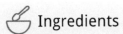 Ingredients

- 1 large celery root, peeled washed and chopped into 1-inch chunks
- 2 tbsp nut milk
- 1 tbsp butter
- 1/4 tsp onion powder
- 1/4 tsp garlic powder
- Salt and pepper to taste

Instructions

1. Steam celery root until completely softened. Move to a mixing bowl. Add all remaining ingredients. Mash with a potato masher until an even consistency is reached. If mix is a little loose, move to a skillet and sauté gently to evaporate some liquid.

Steamed Green Beans with Garlic and Almonds

Serves 4

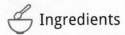 Ingredients

- 4 cups fresh green beans
- 1 tbsp olive oil
- 1 clove garlic, minced
- 2 tbsp slivered almonds
- Salt and pepper to taste

Instructions

1. Steam green beans until crisp tender, about 5 minutes. In a large skillet, sauté garlic in olive oil 2-3 minutes until fragrant. Add beans and almonds and toss to coat. Season with salt and pepper. Serves 4.

Mashed Cauliflower

Serves 4

 Ingredients

- 1 head cauliflower chopped into florets
- 1/4 cup unsweetened almond milk
- 1/2 tsp salt
- 1/4 tsp freshly cracked black pepper
- 1 tbsp chopped chives
- 1 tbsp olive oil
- 1 tsp fresh basil, finely minced

Instructions

1. Steam cauliflower until completely tender.
2. In a small saucepan combine all other ingredients and heat through, being careful not to allow liquid to come to a boil.
3. As soon as liquids are hot, move all ingredients to a large bowl and mash with a potato masher until the desired consistency is reached.
4. If additional liquid is needed add chicken stock 1 tbsp at a time.

Braised Spinach

Serves 4

 Ingredients

- 1 lb fresh spinach
- 2 tbsp water
- 1/2 tsp salt

Instructions

1. Wash spinach and shake off excess moisture. Preheat a large skillet on medium heat until water dropped in pan sizzles. Add spinach. Stir, cooking until spinach wilts and liquid is evaporated. Add additional water if necessary to wilt spinach. Add salt and pepper to taste. Serves 4.

Zucchini and Squash "Noodles"

Serves 4

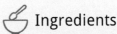 Ingredients

- 3 medium zucchini
- 3 medium yellow squash
- Salt and pepper
- 4 tbsp parmesan cheese

Instructions

1. Wash vegetables and trim off stem end and blossom end. Using a spiralizer or julienne peeler cut all vegetables into long noodle shapes. Blanch in boiling water 1-2 minutes. Drain well, place on 4 plates, and serve with a drizzle of olive oil and sprinkle of herbs of your choice. Top each serving with grated parmesan cheese. The produce section of your local Whole Foods Market may also carry these vegetable noodles. Serves 4.

Grilled Raddichio

Serves 4

Ingredients

- 1 large head of radicchio, quartered through the core end to maintain the structure
- 1 tbsp olive oil
- Salt and freshly ground black pepper
- 1/4 cup balsamic vinegar

Instructions

1. Wash radicchio and shake off excess water. Brush radicchio with olive oil.

2. Preheat a grill pan on medium high heat. Place radicchio on grill pan and cook 3-4 minutes per side until wilted. Season with salt and pepper and drizzle with balsamic vinegar. Serves 4

Garden Salad

Serves 4

Ingredients

- 6 cups shredded lettuce
- 4 cups shredded kale
- 2 cups fresh spinach
- 1/2 cup shredded carrot
- 1 large Roma tomato, halved, then each half cut into thirds
- 4 thin slices of red onion
- 1/2 small cucumber, sliced
- 1/4 cup organic Italian dressing (or other dressing of choice)

Instructions

1. Combine all ingredients except tomato in a large salad bowl. Drizzle with dressing, and toss until coated. Serve in 2-cup servings with 1 wedge of tomato per bowl.

Dijon Mustard Sauce

Serves 4

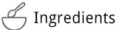

Ingredients

- 1 cup dry white wine
- 3/4 cup chicken stock
- 2 tbsp Dijon mustard
- 1 tbsp stone ground mustard
- 1/4 cup full fat coconut milk
- 1/4 tsp salt

Instructions

1. In a small saucepan simmer wine and stock together until reduced by half. Add mustard and whisk to combine. Stir in coconut milk and salt and heat through.

Baked Winter Squash

Serves 4

 Ingredients

- 1 winter squash such as butternut, acorn, or kabocha
- 1 cup each pecans, cooked multicolor quinoa, chopped mushrooms
- 1 small tart apple, peeled, cored, and chopped
- 1/4 cup dried, fruit-juice sweetened cranberries
- 1 small diced sweet onion
- 2 cloves of garlic
- 2 tbsp liquid aminos or soy sauce
- 2 tsp rubbed sage
- 2 tsp chopped rosemary
- 2 tbsp olive oil
- Sea salt and pepper

Instructions

1. Cut squash in half, scoop out seeds and strings. Brush the exposed flesh with olive oil and season with salt and pepper. Place in a large glass baking dish. Roast in a 425 degree oven until tender while you make the stuffing, 30 to 50 minutes or longer depending on the size of the squash. In a skillet, fry onion until translucent and it is just starting to caramelize. Add garlic and mushrooms and fry until tender. Deglaze with liquid aminos and continue to cook until liquid is absorbed. Add apples, dried cranberries, nuts, quinoa, and herbs and stir to combine. Remove from skillet and place in a large bowl. Let the squash cool for 10 minutes then scoop out the squash from its shells and place in the bowl with the other ingredients. Stir to combine. Spoon the mixture into the squash shells and place in the oven at 350 degrees for 20 minutes.

Confetti Rice Salad

Serves 4

🥣 Ingredients

- 3 cups steamed, cooled brown rice
- 1 cup diced mixed mini red, yellow, and orange peppers
- 1/4 cup chopped chives
- 1 cup fresh peas
- 1/2 cup diced carrots
- 2 tbsp olive oil
- 1/4 cup balsamic or red wine vinegar
- 1/2 tsp salt
- 1/8 tsp cracked black pepper

🍵 Instructions

1. In a large bowl, toss rice, peppers, chives, carrots, and peas together. In a small bowl whisk together oil and vinegar. Season with salt and pepper. Drizzle dressing over salad, mix well to combine. Refrigerate at least 30 minutes before serving.

Brown and Wild Rice Medley

Serves 10

🥣 Ingredients

- 1 cup brown rice
- 1 cup wild rice
- 4 cups chicken or vegetable stock
- 1 clove garlic
- 1 tsp onion powder
- 1/2 tsp rosemary
- 1/2 tsp thyme

🍵 Instructions

1. Bring stock and seasonings to a boil. Add brown and wild rice. Cover and reduce to a simmer. Cook 45 minutes until liquid is mostly absorbed. Turn off heat and allow to sit, covered for 15 minutes. Fluff with a fork before serving. Serves 10.

Creamy Cilantro Lime Slaw

Serves 6-8

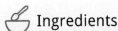 Ingredients

- 2 cups shredded green cabbage
- 2 cups shredded red cabbage
- 1 cup shredded carrots
- 1/2 cup chopped parsley
- 1/2 cup chopped fresh cilantro
- 1/2 cup chopped green onions

Dressing:
- 2 tbsp sour cream
- 1/4 cup extra virgin olive oil
- Juice of 2 limes
- 2 tbsp honey
- 1 clove garlic, crushed and minced
- Salt to taste

Instructions

1. Toss all vegetables and herbs in a large bowl until well combined. In a screw top jar add all dressing ingredients, cover tightly, and shake well to combine. Drizzle half of the dressing over the slaw, toss well, then add remaining dressing and toss again. Allow to rest in the refrigerator for at least 30 minutes prior to serving for flavors to combine. Serves 6-8.

Citrus Brown Rice

Serves 4

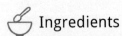 Ingredients

- 1 cup brown rice
- 1 1/2 cups water
- 1/4 cup orange juice
- 1/4 cup lemon juice
- 1 tsp each orange and lemon zest
- 1/2 tsp salt

Instructions

1. Bring water and juice to a boil, add zest, salt, and rice. Cover and simmer 40 minutes. Turn off flame and let sit for 10 minutes. Fluff with a fork before serving.

Desserts

Gluten-Free Tahini Cookies

Gluten-Free Almond Flour Brownies

Serves 4

 Ingredients

- 3/4 cup almond flour
- 2/3 cup raw honey
- 5 tbsp unsweetened cocoa powder
- 2 eggs
- 1/4 cup melted butter
- 1 tsp vanilla extract
- 1/2 cup chopped walnuts, optional

Instructions

1. Preheat oven to 325 degrees.

2. Grease a square glass 8 x 8 inch pan. Dust with almond flour.

3. Whisk almond flour, honey, cocoa powder, eggs, butter, and vanilla extract in a large bowl. Fold in walnuts if desired. Pour into greased pan. Smooth the top of the batter.

4. Baked in preheated oven for about 20 to 25 minutes or until a toothpick inserted in the center comes out clean or at least does not have any wet batter stuck to it.

Grain-Free Peanut Butter Ginger Cookies

Makes
about 14

 Ingredients

- 1 cup organic, unsweetened peanut butter
- 3/4 cup organic stevia
- 1 tbsp honey
- 1 tsp vanilla extract
- 1 large egg, lightly beaten
- 2 tsp finely grated fresh ginger

Instructions

1. Preheat oven to 350 degrees.

2. In a medium bowl, combine peanut butter, stevia, honey, vanilla, and egg. Stir in ginger.

3. Line baking sheet with parchment paper. Roll dough into 1-inch balls and place on parchment paper about 1 inch apart. Flatten the dough using a fork to make criss-cross patterns.

4. Bake until golden brown around the edges, about 10 minutes. Let cool on baking sheet for 3 minutes, then transfer to a wire rack to cool completely. Makes about 14 cookies.

Berry Salad

Serves 4

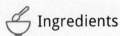 Ingredients

- 2 cups sliced strawberries
- 1 cup blueberries
- 1 cup raspberries
- 1 cup blackberries
- ¼ cup chopped, roasted pecans
- Juice of one lemon

Instructions

1. Combine berries in a large bowl. Stir in pecans. Sprinkle with lemon juice and stir.

Gluten-Free Tahini Cookies

Makes
about 14

 Ingredients

- 1/2 cup butter
- 1/2 cup honey
- 1/2 cup tahini
- 1 tsp vanilla extract
- 1/2 tsp baking soda
- Pinch of salt
- 1 1/4 cups gluten-free flour
- 5 tbsp sesame seeds

Instructions

1. In a large bowl, cream the butter and honey. Mix in tahini and vanilla extract.

2. In a medium bowl, whisk together baking soda, salt, and flour. Add to tahini mixture and combine.

3. Roll dough into 1 tbsp balls and place on a cookie sheet covered in parchment paper.

4. Using the bottom of a glass dusted with gluten-free flour, press down onto the cookies until they're 1/3 inch thick. Sprinkle with sesame seeds.

5. Refrigerate for 15 minutes then bake in a preheated 350 degree oven for about 10 minutes until the cookies are a light golden brown.

6. Let cookies cool on the baking sheet for 10 minutes then transfer to a wire rack.

Fruit Salad with Dates and Mint

Serves 4

 ## Ingredients

- 1 cup blueberries
- 1 cup chopped apples, skin on
- 1 cup orange slices, seeded
- 1 cup sliced strawberries
- 1/4 cup chopped dates
- 2 Tbs chopped fresh mint leaves
- 1 teaspoon lemon juice
- A few sprinkles of cinnamon

Instructions

1. Chop the apples, slice the strawberries, and seed the orange slices and place in large bowl together with the blueberries.

2. Chop the dates and add to the fruit. Chop the mint leaves and add to the bowl.

3. Sprinkle the lemon juice over the fruit and other contents.

4. Toss everything together in the bowl. Sprinkle cinnamon over the fruit mixture.

Chia Pudding with Blackberries and Blueberries

Serves 4

Ingredients

- 2 cups full fat coconut milk
- 1/2 cup chia seeds
- 1/2 tsp vanilla extract
- 1/4 cup organic stevia
- 1/2 cup fresh blueberries
- 1/2 cup fresh blackberries
- 1 tsp raw local honey

Instructions

1. Add all ingredients except honey, blueberries, and blackberries to a blender and blend for 1-2 minutes until smooth. Pour into the medium bowl.

2. Divide into 4 portions in small airtight containers. Refrigerate overnight stirring a few times in the first hour to maintain even thickening.

3. Toss blueberries and blackberries with honey and seal in an airtight container.

4. In the morning top pudding with 1/4 cup of mixed fruit and stir to combine.

Mixed Fresh Fruit Bowl

Serves 6

 Ingredients

- 2 bananas
- 2, 15 oz cans unsweetened mandarin oranges
- 1 medium apple
- 2 cups seedless grapes
  12 dates
- 1 cup chopped walnuts
- 1 5 oz cup plain Greek yogurt
- 1 tbsp honey
- 1 tbsp lime juice
- 2 tbsp lemon juice in 1 cup water

Instructions

1. Drain mandarin oranges in a colander while preparing the rest of the salad. Place 2 tbsp lemon juice in 1 cup of water in a small bowl. Wash apple and grapes and pat dry. Add grapes to a large serving bowl. Core and thinly slice apple, dipping the slices in the lemon juice and water to prevent browning. Add to serving bowl. Slice bananas into 1/4-inch thick coins and dip in lemon juice and water to prevent browning. Add to bowl. Chop dates and sprinkle over the top.

2. In a small separate bowl whisk together lime juice, honey, and yogurt. Pour over salad and toss well to coat. Add mandarin oranges and fold carefully to coat without breaking the sections. Just before serving sprinkle chopped walnuts on top. Serves 6.

About the Authors

Dr. Chris D. Meletis is an educator, international author and lecturer. His personal mission is "Changing World's Health One Person at a Time." He believes that when people become educated about their body, that is the moment when change begins. He has authored over a dozen books and in excess of 200 national scientific articles in such journals and magazines as *Natural Health, Alternative and Complementary Therapies, Townsend Letter for Doctors and Patients, Life Extension, and Natural Pharmacy.*

Dr. Meletis served as Dean of Naturopathic Medicine and Chief Medical Officer for 7 years at the oldest Naturopathic Medical School in North America. He was awarded the 2003 physician of the year by the American Association of Naturopathic Physicians. He has a deep passion for helping the underprivileged and spearheaded the creation of 16 free natural medicine healthcare clinics in the Portland metropolitan area of Oregon.

Kimberly Wilkes has written about health and nutrition for 20 years. She has published more than 500 articles as a co-author with healthcare practitioners or under her own byline. Her articles have appeared in such publications as *Whole Health Insider, Townsend Letter, Vitamin Research News,* and the *Integrative Medicine Journal.* She first started eating a gluten-free and sugar-free diet when she was diagnosed with a skin condition (rosacea) in 1998. After switching to the diet, her rosacea disappeared and she now has glowing, healthy skin.

Alphabetical Recipe Index

Made in the USA
Coppell, TX
16 May 2020